THE SKINNY air fryer COOKBOOK

THE BEST RECIPES FOR **CUTTING THE FAT** AND **KEEPING THE FLAVOR** IN YOUR FAVORITE FRIED FOODS

ella sanders

CASTLE POINT BOOKS
NEW YORK

www.castlepointbooks.com

The Castle Point Books trademark is owned by Castle Point Publishing, LLC.
Castle Point books are published and distributed by St. Martin's Publishing Group.

ISBN 978-1-250-27952-1 (paper-over-board)
eISBN 978-1-250-27953-8 (ebook)

Design by Joanna Williams
Production by Laura White
Photography under license from Shutterstock.com
except photo on page 39 by Allan Penn

Our books may be purchased in bulk for promotional, educational, or business use.

Please contact your local bookseller or the Macmillan Corporate
and Premium Sales Department at 1-800-221-7945, extension 5442,
or by email at MacmillanSpecialMarkets@macmillan.com.

First Edition: 2022

10 9 8 7 6 5 4 3 2 1

contents

4

get the skinny

9

good mornings

27

quick bites

45

weeknight dinners

97

easy entertaining

117

sweet treats

139

index

get the skinny

Whether you want to drop 5 pounds or 50, focusing on what you eat is the best way to lose weight safely and effectively. In fact, research suggests that cooking at home may be the easiest strategy for realizing the benefits of enjoying healthier meals. You can better control which ingredients you use as well as portion sizes. But what about cooking methods? Does that mean you'll have to subsist on a lifetime of smoothies and steamed vegetables? Not if you have an air fryer!

Your air fryer is hands down the most useful kitchen appliance to help you reach your weight loss goals because it can help you enjoy familiar flavors without the added fats that come with cooking methods like traditional frying. This cookbook is filled with more than 75 delicious recipes designed to satisfy without weighing you down. You'll love skinny dishes like Chicken Parmigiana (page 62), Spicy Sicilian Chicken Drumsticks (page 102), Crab Cakes with Roasted Corn-Pepper Relish (page 114), Ham and Cheese Calzones (page 73), and Guilt-Free Veggie Egg Rolls (page 38). And you can enjoy sweet but smart indulgences with skinny desserts like Glazed Doughnuts (page 119), Peanut

Butter Chocolate Chip Cookies (page 125), and Chocolate Lava Cake for Two (page 126). Your air fryer makes it easy to get big flavor with skinny results—it's your secret weapon for weight loss!

benefits of your air fryer

If weight loss is your goal, an air fryer can be such a valuable asset in the kitchen. The benefits you get with an air fryer that can also make losing weight easier include:

Less fat. Air fryers circulate hot air to cook foods, resulting in the same crisp exterior and tender interior produced by conventional deep fryers but with far less fat. Beyond frying, the air fryer can also roast, steam, grill, and bake. Whatever cooking method you turn to the air fryer for, it improves the process with faster, more even heat—and delicious results.

Speedy cooking. Not only do air fryers tend to speed the cooking time for most recipes (the circulation of hot air means foods cook faster), but you'll also find that using an air fryer usually involves less hassle than traditional cooking methods. So you'll stick with all of the super-easy recipes in this book. Need to check for doneness? Just slide open the basket to take a quick look. Need to turn the food to ensure even baking? Give the basket a quick shake. That said, models vary, so use the cooking times in this collection as a guide versus a rule and adjust accordingly.

Less mess. Air frying is considerably less messy than deep-fat frying. The units are self-contained, so you don't need to contend with splatters. And because most air fryer baskets come with a nonstick coating, cleanup is a breeze. You'll find more time to get out and enjoy an active lifestyle instead of doing dishes. Just be sure to always follow your manufacturer's safety instructions for proper care and cleaning of your air fryer.

Comfort and convenience. Baking with a conventional oven during the summer months is a surefire way to heat up your whole kitchen in a hurry. It's tempting to turn to takeout. But given their compact size, air fryers simply don't give off as much heat. Many models also come with preset features for baking certain types of foods at the press of a button, and some manufacturers now offer air fryers that do double duty as pressure cookers, too. At the end of the day, there are few things that you can make in a conventional oven that you can't make more easily in an air fryer. The only challenge is that sometimes you may need to cook a recipe in batches because the units are obviously smaller. That's simple enough and could even help you stay on track with portions when it comes to making cookies and other dessert batches.

the recipe for weight loss

Every gram of fat and calorie you can cut with the help of your air fryer adds up! Losing weight is a numbers game. Essentially, once you figure out how many calories your body normally burns, make a plan to consume about 500 calories fewer every day and you can look forward to a steady weight loss of a pound a week. There are plenty of online tools to help you calculate your basal metabolic rate (the calories your body needs for basic functions like breathing and keeping your heart beating). These sites also consider your starting size and estimated activity level to help you figure out the total number of calories your body uses.

Keep in mind that the sweet spot for weight loss lies in between your basal metabolic rate and total calories burned in a day.

Severely limiting your calorie intake can actually wreak havoc on your metabolism and cause your body to conserve calories. So make a goal that is realistic, safe, and attainable. Beyond counting calories, these totally manageable strategies can also help power your weight loss.

Focus on fat. One gram of fat contains 9 calories, more than twice the calories you get from 1 gram of protein or carbohydrates, which means that paying careful attention to your ingredients as well as the fats you use in your cooking is a great way to manage your total calorie

HELPFUL KITCHEN TOOLS

In general, you can use any glass, metal, or silicone baking dishes with your air fryer as long as they fit in the basket and don't block the circulation of hot air. Here are some other key items you'll want to have on hand to help you use your air fryer for weight loss:

Kitchen scale: Weighing your food is the best way to make sure your portion sizes stay on track. With a digital scale, you can know exactly how big that piece of meat really is.

Olive oil spray: Instead of using nonstick cooking spray, which may over time compromise the integrity of nonstick surfaces, consider purchasing a pump-style spray bottle that you can fill with regular olive oil. Some foods, especially those with a breaded coating, will benefit from a light coating of oil before air frying. If you prefer a neutral-flavored oil, avocado oil is an excellent choice.

Parchment paper: Treated with a thin layer of silicone, parchment paper provides a nonstick surface for delicate foods that might otherwise slip through the holes of your air fryer basket. When lining your basket with parchment, avoid cutting a piece so large that it covers all the holes (otherwise air will not circulate properly).

Meat thermometer: While the recipes in this collection offer visual hints to explain what your food should look like when it's done, the only way to know for sure whether meats are cooked to a safe temperature is to rely on a meat thermometer.

Tongs: Although it's possible to simply give many foods a quick shake in the basket to ensure even cooking, some foods require deliberate turning. Tongs are helpful for this task.

intake. However, all fats are not created equal. Some, like the monounsaturated fats found in olive oil and nuts, are considered heart-healthy foods because they play an important role in controlling inflammation. In general, try to minimize saturated fats (abundant in red meats and full-fat dairy products). Most experts advise steering clear of trans fats (the kind that manufacturers use in processed foods) altogether.

Don't skimp on protein. Protein is the building block your body needs to build muscle, and it plays an important role in helping to control your appetite and keep your metabolism humming. However, the challenge is that many protein-rich foods are also high in fats, so opt for leaner sources like seafood and poultry whenever feasible. It's also helpful to keep in mind what a healthy serving size looks. A serving of chicken breast, for example, is about the size of the palm of your hand or a deck of playing cards.

Be careful with carbs. Carbohydrates help your body perform many functions, but where weight loss is concerned it's helpful to think of carbs as a kind of fuel supply that comes in several different grades. Simple carbohydrates (think sugar and white bread) are like low-grade fuel sources that your body burns quickly, which can lead to spikes in both glucose and hunger levels. Complex carbohydrates, on the other hand, are like a high-grade fuel that your body burns more slowly. Whole grains, fruits, and vegetables are all forms of complex carbohydrates that offer many other valuable nutrients and should be the main source of carbohydrates in a healthy weight loss eating plan.

Get more fiber and drink plenty of water. Complex carbohydrates contain fiber, the indigestible part of plants that keep things moving efficiently through your system. When you're trying to lose weight, fiber is especially beneficial because it helps you feel full longer. Aim for 25 grams of fiber a day. And while you're at it, make sure you're drinking at least 8 glasses of water, too, because dehydration is often the culprit behind the temptation to overeat.

With your air fryer and these smart eating approaches, you can make your favorite foods lighter and weight loss easy. Ready to dig in? Every recipe in the chapters that follow includes nutritional information—calories, fat, protein, and more—to help you stay on track with your goals. And every dish has been designed with your air fryer and weight loss in mind, so eating skinny becomes almost automatic. Start enjoying amazing meals and even luscious desserts while making your way toward a new you—your air fryer is the secret!

good mornings

Small-Batch Granola **10**

Cherry-Oatmeal Bars **13**

French Toast Cups with Raspberries **14**

Apple Dutch Baby Pancake **15**

Cheesy Bacon & Egg Cups **16**

Sunny-Side-Up Eggs in Avocado **19**

English Muffin Breakfast Pizzas **20**

Berry Creamy Breakfast Sandwiches **21**

Skinny Chilaquiles **22**

Big Easy Sweet Potato Hash **24**

Cheesy Sausage Biscuit Balls **25**

Small-Batch Granola

Makes 4 servings • Prep time: 10 minutes • Total time: 1 hour 10 minutes

3 tablespoons canola oil

3 tablespoons honey

½ teaspoon vanilla extract

¼ teaspoon ground cinnamon

¼ teaspoon salt

1½ cups rolled oats

¼ cup pecans or walnuts, coarsely chopped

¼ cup raisins or other dried fruit

Your air fryer is golden for making crunchy granola in perfect portions! Going homemade also gives you control of the ingredients and calories—store-bought granola can be loaded with extra sugar and fat. All it takes is 10 minutes of hands-on time while your appliance does the rest to give you a great breakfast that you can take on the go.

1. Preheat the air fryer to 250°F. Cut a piece of parchment paper to fit inside the air fryer basket.

2. In a large bowl, combine the oil, honey, vanilla, cinnamon, and salt. Stir until smooth. Add the oats and nuts and stir until the mixture is thoroughly combined.

3. Spread the oat mixture on the parchment paper to an even thickness.

4. Air fry for 1 hour, or until golden throughout. Remove from the air fryer and allow to fully cool. Break the granola into bite-size pieces if necessary, stir in the raisins, and store in a covered container for up to a week.

TIP: When assembling ingredients, be sure to measure the canola oil first. The little bit of oil remaining in your measuring spoon will ensure the honey slides out easily.

Per ½-cup serving: 330 calories, 5 g protein, 42 g carbohydrates, 17 g fat (1.5 g sat fat), 4 g fiber

Cherry-Oatmeal Bars

Makes 12 bars • Prep time: 15 minutes • Total time: 50 minutes + cooling time

4 tablespoons unsalted butter

1 cup rolled oats

½ cup all-purpose flour

¼ cup packed light brown sugar

¼ teaspoon ground ginger

¼ teaspoon kosher salt

½ cup all-fruit cherry preserves

Enjoy the goodness of oatmeal beyond the bowl! These breakfast bars sandwich luscious fruit filling between two layers of a satisfying crumble crust for a portable breakfast the whole family will love. It's easy to adjust the recipe to your favorite flavor of fruit preserves.

1. Preheat the air fryer to 370°F. Line an 8 x 8-inch baking pan with parchment paper so that the paper overhangs two sides like handles.

2. In a large microwave-safe bowl, melt the butter in the microwave on high for 1 minute. Add the oats, flour, brown sugar, ginger, and salt. Stir until thoroughly combined and forms clumps. Set aside ½ cup of the crumble mixture, then press the rest into an even layer in the bottom of the prepared pan.

3. Spread the preserves evenly over the crust. Sprinkle the reserved oat mixture evenly over the top.

4. Air fry the bars for 35 to 40 minutes, until the topping is golden. Place the pan on a wire rack to cool completely before slicing.

TIP: This recipe works best if your air fryer can accommodate an 8 x 8-inch pan. If necessary, use an 8-inch round pan instead and cut the bars into wedges.

Per bar: 120 calories, 2 g protein, 13 g carbohydrates, 4 g fat (2.5 g sat fat), 1 g fiber

French Toast Cups with Raspberries

Makes 2 servings • Prep time: 15 minutes • Total time: 35 minutes + chilling time

2 slices Italian bread (about 2 ounces), cut into ½-inch cubes, divided

½ cup fresh or frozen raspberries

2 ounces fat-free cream cheese, cut into ¼-inch cubes

2 large eggs

½ cup reduced-fat 2% milk

3 tablespoons light pancake syrup, divided

½ teaspoon vanilla extract

You can have the classic taste of French toast without standing over a hot skillet or breaking the calorie bank. Your air fryer makes it simple! To keep your breakfast skinny, go for light pancake syrup. Most brands of light have about half the calories of regular syrup, but you're unlikely to taste much of a difference in this dish because the bright flavor of the raspberries shines through.

1. Coat two 8-ounce custard cups with nonstick spray.

2. Put one quarter of the bread cubes in each custard cup. Sprinkle the bread with the raspberries and cream cheese cubes. Top with the remaining bread.

3. In a small bowl, whisk together the eggs, milk, 1 tablespoon of the syrup, and vanilla. Pour the mixture over the bread. Cover and refrigerate for at least 1 hour.

4. Preheat the air fryer to 325°F. Place the custard cups in the air fryer basket. Air fry for 12 to 15 minutes, until golden brown and puffed.

5. Serve drizzled with the remaining 2 tablespoons of syrup.

Per serving: 260 calories, 16 g protein, 33 g carbohydrates, 7 g fat (2.8 g sat fat), 3 g fiber

Apple Dutch Baby Pancake

Makes 2 servings • Prep time: 10 minutes • Total time: 55 minutes

¼ cup all-purpose flour

4 tablespoons sugar, divided

¼ teaspoon baking powder

¼ teaspoon ground cinnamon

Pinch of salt

½ cup reduced-fat 2% milk

2 large eggs

½ teaspoon vanilla extract

1 tablespoon unsalted butter

1 small Granny Smith apple, cored and thinly sliced

2 tablespoons light pancake syrup

Turn off the oven and forget simmering apples on the stovetop, as the traditional version of this recipe usually requires. All of your ingredients for this luscious dish come together easily (and deliciously!) in your air fryer. At 320 calories per serving, it only tastes rich!

1. In a bowl, stir together the flour, 2 tablespoons of the sugar, baking powder, cinnamon, and salt until combined.

2. In a separate bowl, stir together the milk, eggs, and vanilla until combined. Whisk the milk mixture lightly, then slowly add the flour mixture, whisking constantly, until thoroughly combined. Let the batter stand for 30 minutes.

3. Preheat the air fryer to 400°F.

4. Place the butter in a 6-inch round baking pan and air fry for 1 minute until the butter is melted and the pan is hot.

5. Brush some of the butter up the sides of the pan and sprinkle 1 tablespoon of sugar over the butter. Arrange the apple slices in the pan in a single layer. Sprinkle the remaining 1 tablespoon of sugar over the apples. Air fry for 2 minutes or until the mixture bubbles.

6. Gently pour the batter mixture over the apples. Reduce the air fryer temperature to 350°F and air fry for 12 minutes, or until the batter is golden brown around the edges and the center is cooked through. Serve drizzled with the pancake syrup.

Per serving: 320 calories, 8 g protein, 57 g carbohydrates, 7 g fat (4.4 g sat fat), 2 g fiber

Cheesy Bacon & Egg Cups

Makes 4 servings • Prep time: 10 minutes • Total time: 22 minutes

4 large eggs

Salt and freshly ground black pepper

2 ounces Canadian bacon, chopped

¼ red bell pepper, finely chopped

½ cup reduced-fat shredded Cheddar cheese, divided

1 tablespoon chopped fresh chives (optional)

What's better than an omelet? A medley of favorite breakfast flavors with no pan watching or tricky flipping required! This recipe twist also renders the egg dish perfectly portable for a grab-and-go breakfast. And you have so many options—try adding a different cheese or choice of chopped veggie.

1. Preheat the air fryer to 400°F. Lightly coat 4 silicone muffin cups with vegetable oil.

2. In a bowl, whisk the eggs and season with salt and pepper. Add the bacon, bell pepper, and half of the cheese. Mix until the ingredients are thoroughly combined. Divide the egg mixture among the muffin cups and top with the remaining cheese.

3. Air fry for 12 to 15 minutes, or until cooked through. Top with fresh chives (if using).

TIP: Silicone baking cups are especially useful to have on hand because they are reusable and offer a little flexibility if space is tight in your air fryer.

Per serving: 130 calories, 13 g protein, 1 g carbohydrates, 8 g fat (3.3 g sat fat), 0 g fiber

Sunny-Side-Up Eggs in Avocado

Makes 2 servings • Prep time: 5 minutes • Total time: 14 minutes

1 Haas avocado, halved and pitted

2 large eggs

Salt and freshly ground black pepper

Chopped fresh parsley, for garnish (optional)

1 lime, cut into wedges (optional)

Avocado toast has won many hearts, but avocado eggs are even more satisfying! The first time you make them, take careful note of how much time your air fryer requires to cook them to the level of doneness that you prefer. Once you've nailed that detail, future batches are a cinch to make. If your menu plan includes carbs, serve with a side of toast.

1. Preheat the air fryer to 400°F.

2. Slice off a thin portion off the rounded bottom of each avocado half so that it will sit solidly in the air fryer basket without rolling around.

3. Break an egg directly into the hollow of each avocado half.

4. Air fry for 9 minutes, pausing halfway through the cooking time to see if the egg whites are set and the yolk has reached the desired doneness.

5. Season to taste with salt and pepper and garnish with chopped parsley (if using). Serve with lime wedges (if using).

Per serving: 185 calories, 8 g protein, 6 g carbohydrates, 15 g fat (3 g sat fat), 5 g fiber

English Muffin Breakfast Pizzas

Makes 2 servings • Prep time: 5 minutes • Total time: 15 minutes

2 whole-grain English muffins, split

1 Roma tomato, thinly sliced

Salt and freshly ground black pepper

½ cup shredded part-skim mozzarella cheese

2 vegetarian breakfast sausage patties, crumbled

Pinch of dried oregano

Craving a cold slice for breakfast? These toasted breakfast pizzas are a much better choice, loaded with a healthy balance of protein and fiber to get your morning off to a great start. If you need to take your morning meal on the road, simply turn your portion of two mini pizzas into a breakfast sandwich.

1. Preheat the air fryer to 400°F.

2. Arrange the muffins halves cut side up in the air fryer basket. Air fry for 3 minutes until warm.

3. Season the tomatoes to taste with salt and pepper. Set the tomato slices on top of the muffins and scatter equal amounts of cheese and sausage on top, followed by a dash of oregano.

4. Continue air frying for 5 minutes until the cheese is melted and beginning to brown.

Per serving: 285 calories, 21 g protein, 32 g carbohydrates, 9 g fat (3.4 g sat fat), 6 g fiber

Berry Creamy Breakfast Sandwiches

Makes 4 servings • Prep time: 10 minutes • Total time: 15 minutes

4 ounces soft goat cheese

1 tablespoon honey

8 slices whole wheat bread

1 cup blackberries

Turn up the flavor and nutrition on your basic jelly toast! Blackberries boast an impressive amount of fiber (8 grams per cup), and they work especially well in this sandwich because they hold their shape better than other berries when cooked. Of course, if you're a die-hard fan of another type of berry, feel free to substitute your favorite fruit. The lightly sweetened goat cheese pairs well with just about everything.

1. Preheat the air fryer to 350°F.

2. In a small bowl, use a fork to mash the goat cheese and honey into a smooth spread. Divide the cheese mixture among the bread slices and spread evenly almost to the edges.

3. Distribute the berries over 4 slices of bread and top with the remaining slices. Lightly spritz the sandwiches with a neutral-flavored cooking oil, such as avocado oil.

4. Working in batches if necessary, arrange the sandwiches in the air fryer basket so they are not touching. Air fry for 5 to 7 minutes, or until toasted.

Per serving: 285 calories, 14 g protein, 35 g carbohydrates, 10 g fat (6.1 g sat fat), 4 g fiber

Skinny Chilaquiles

Makes 1 serving • Prep time: 5 minutes • Total time: 15 minutes

3 (6-inch) corn tortillas

Pinch of kosher salt

½ cup green enchilada sauce

1 teaspoon unsalted butter

1 large egg

¼ red onion, thinly sliced

1 tablespoon crumbled Cotija cheese

Hot sauce, for serving (optional)

Using your air fryer to toast the tortillas is an easy way to prepare this dish with far less oil than if you use regular fried chips. If you have two hungry people in the house, there's no need to prepare a second batch. Just cook another egg and warm up a cup of black beans to share alongside and you'll both enjoy a 310-calorie breakfast instead.

1. Preheat the air fryer to 360°F.

2. Lightly spritz both sides of each tortilla with olive oil and sprinkle with salt. Stack the tortillas and cut into 6 wedges. Scatter the tortillas in the air fryer basket so there is room for the air to circulate. Air fry for 5 minutes, pausing halfway to shake the basket, until the chips begin to brown.

3. Transfer the chips to a large bowl and top with the enchilada sauce, tossing until the chips are thoroughly coated. Return the chips to the air fryer basket and air fry 3 minutes longer until lightly browned.

4. Meanwhile, heat the butter in a small skillet over medium heat and cook the egg to your desired doneness.

5. Transfer the chips to a plate and top with the egg, onion slices, cheese, and a dash of hot sauce (if using).

Per serving: 385 calories, 14 g protein, 39 g carbohydrates, 20 g fat (9.8 g sat fat), 6 g fiber

Big Easy Sweet Potato Hash

Makes 2 servings • Prep time: 5 minutes • Total time: 15 minutes

1 large sweet potato (about 12 ounces), peeled and chopped

¼ red onion, chopped

¼ red bell pepper, seeded and chopped

1 tablespoon olive oil

1 teaspoon Cajun seasoning

1 (3-ounce) andouille sausage, chopped

2 tablespoons chopped fresh parsley

Let the good times roll with the bold flavors in this Cajun version of a classic breakfast hash. With 6 grams of fiber per serving, it's practically guilt-free! If andouille sausage is unavailable, substitute turkey kielbasa in its place. Both work equally well in an air fryer.

1. Preheat the air fryer to 400°F.

2. In a large bowl, combine the sweet potato, onion, and bell pepper. Drizzle with the oil and sprinkle with the Cajun seasoning. Toss to coat.

3. Transfer the mixture to the air fryer basket and air fry for 10 minutes.

4. Add the sausage and shake the basket. Air fry 10 minutes longer until the sausage is sizzling and the sweet potatoes are fork-tender and beginning to brown.

5. Top with the parsley before serving.

Per serving: 295 calories, 11 g protein, 37 g carbohydrates, 12 g fat (3 g sat fat), 6 g fiber

Cheesy Sausage Biscuit Balls

Makes 6 servings • Prep time: 15 minutes • Total time: 22 minutes

1 pound 93% lean ground turkey

1 teaspoon salt

1 teaspoon rubbed sage

½ teaspoon freshly ground black pepper

½ teaspoon onion powder

¼ teaspoon red pepper flakes (optional)

2 cups shredded reduced-fat Cheddar cheese

1½ cups biscuit mix, such as Bisquick

These tasty breakfast balls are considerably lighter than the popular version you may recall with regular pork sausage and processed cheese. Best of all, if you make a batch ahead of time you can reheat them in the air fryer in a few minutes flat. Perfect for busy mornings!

1. Preheat the air fryer to 400°F.

2. In a large bowl, combine the turkey, salt, sage, black pepper, onion powder, and red pepper flakes (if using). Mix gently until thoroughly combined. Add the cheese and biscuit mix and stir again until combined. Shape the mixture into 1¼-inch balls.

3. Working in batches if necessary, arrange the balls in a single layer in the air fryer basket; spritz lightly with olive oil. Air fry for 7 to 10 minutes, pausing halfway through the cooking time to shake the basket, until lightly browned and a meat thermometer inserted into the center of a ball reaches 165°F.

TIP: Rubbed sage is dried sage leaves that have been rubbed into a fine, fluffy powder. It's less concentrated so a teaspoon of rubbed sage will be less intense than a teaspoon of ground sage.

Per serving: *350 calories, 27 g protein, 20 g carbohydrates, 18 g fat (7.2 g sat fat), 1 g fiber*

quick bites

Fried Cauliflower with Spicy Dipping Sauce 29

Herbed Ricotta Bites 30

Healthier Mozzarella Sticks 31

Cabbage Patties with Zucchini 32

Perfect Steak Fries 35

Sweet Onion Rings 36

Guilt-Free Veggie Egg Rolls 38

Crab Rangoon 39

Bacon-Wrapped Asparagus 41

Smoky Chickpeas 42

Crispy Tofu Bites 43

Fried Cauliflower
with Spicy Dipping Sauce

Makes 4 servings • Prep time: 15 minutes • Total time: 30 minutes

FRIED CAULIFLOWER

4 cups cauliflower florets

1 cup panko breadcrumbs

¼ cup grated Parmesan cheese

1 large egg, beaten

SPICY DIPPING SAUCE

¼ cup light mayonnaise

1 tablespoon sriracha

1 tablespoon fresh lime juice

2 tablespoons chopped fresh cilantro (optional)

Deep-fried cauliflower is hard to resist because the crunchy coating and creamy vegetable inside are an unbeatable combination. But just one floret can contain a whopping 200 calories! Fortunately, you can make this treat considerably lighter in calories—and just as delicious—with an air fryer.

1. To make the fried cauliflower: Blanch the cauliflower in boiling water for 2 to 3 minutes. Drain into a colander and rinse with cold water to stop the cooking process. Pat dry with paper towels to remove as much water as possible.

2. In a shallow bowl, combine the breadcrumbs and cheese. Dip each of the florets into the beaten egg, then into the breadcrumb mixture, coating evenly. Arrange the florets in the air fryer basket, making sure they don't touch, and spritz lightly with olive oil. Set the air fryer to 400°F. Working in batches if necessary, air fry for 10 minutes until golden.

3. To make the spicy dipping sauce: Whisk together the mayonnaise, sriracha, and lime juice in a small bowl until smooth. Top with the cilantro (if using).

Per serving: 210 calories, 5 g protein, 27 g carbohydrates, 8 g fat (1.7 g sat fat), 3 g fiber

Herbed Ricotta Bites

Makes 4 servings • Prep time: 15 minutes • Total time: 23 minutes + chilling time

1 cup part-skim ricotta cheese

2 tablespoons all-purpose flour

½ teaspoon dried thyme

½ teaspoon dried rosemary, crushed

½ teaspoon dried basil

½ teaspoon kosher salt

¼ teaspoon freshly ground pepper

2 large eggs, beaten, divided

1 cup panko breadcrumbs

Cheese doesn't need to be off-limits! Some research suggests that getting an adequate supply of calcium in your diet can boost your weight loss efforts, which makes cheese dishes like this one even easier to enjoy. However, ricotta has an extremely mild flavor, so perking it up with a good combination of herbs is essential.

1. In a medium bowl, stir together the ricotta, flour, thyme, rosemary, basil, salt, pepper, and half of the beaten eggs until thoroughly combined. Scoop approximately 1 tablespoon of the mixture into the palm of your hand and roll into a ball. Repeat with the remaining mixture.

2. Dip each of the balls into the remaining beaten egg and then into the breadcrumbs, coating evenly.

3. Place the balls on a baking sheet and refrigerate for 1 hour.

4. Preheat the air fryer to 400°F. Spritz the balls lightly with olive oil before transferring to the air fryer basket, making sure they don't touch.

5. Working in batches if necessary, air fry 8 to 9 minutes, or until golden.

Per serving: 210 calories, 9 g protein, 26 g carbohydrates, 5 g fat (3 g sat fat), 0 g fiber

Healthier Mozzarella Sticks

Makes 6 servings • Prep time: 10 minutes • Total time: 16 minutes + freezing time

1 (12-ounce/count) package mozzarella string cheese

1½ cups panko breadcrumbs

¼ cup grated Parmesan cheese

¼ cup all-purpose flour

2 large eggs, beaten

If you enjoy ordering deep-fried mozzarella sticks at your favorite restaurant, this recipe is a game changer. One restaurant serving can contain close to 700 calories! These air-fried mozzarella sticks, on the other hand, come in at less than half that number and are just as appetizing.

1. Remove the cheese from the individually wrapped packages and cut in half, or thirds, depending on the length you prefer.

2. Place the sticks on a baking sheet, cover with plastic wrap, and freeze for 2 hours.

3. Preheat the air fryer to 400°F.

4. In a shallow bowl, stir together the breadcrumbs and Parmesan cheese. Place the flour and eggs in separate shallow bowls. Roll the frozen cheese in the flour, followed by the eggs, and finally the breadcrumb–Parmesan mixture. Lightly spritz each prepared stick with olive oil.

5. Arrange the sticks in the air fryer basket, making sure they don't touch. Working in batches if necessary, air fry for 3 minutes, then remove and carefully flip. Air fry for an additional 3 to 4 minutes or until golden.

Per serving: 315 calories, 18 g protein, 27 g carbohydrates, 13 g fat (7.8 g sat fat), 0 g fiber

Cabbage Patties with Zucchini

Makes 2 servings • Prep time: 20 minutes • Total time: 26 minutes

2 cups finely shredded cabbage

1 small zucchini, shredded

1 teaspoon salt

2 scallions, thinly sliced

1 large egg, beaten

½ cup panko breadcrumbs

¼ cup grated Parmesan cheese

1 tablespoon chopped fresh dill, plus additional for garnish

¼ cup reduced-fat sour cream

Air fryers are incredibly handy appliances, but they're not the only time-savers in your kitchen. If your food processor has a slicing or shredding disk, you'll definitely want to use it to prep the veggies in this recipe. Cabbage and zucchini are both low in fat and high in fiber, making them wonder foods that help you feel full on fewer calories.

1. In a large bowl, combine the cabbage and zucchini and sprinkle with the salt. Massage gently until thoroughly combined and let sit for 10 minutes. Line a colander with cheesecloth or a clean tea towel and drain the vegetables into the colander. Gather up the sides of the cloth and squeeze gently to remove as much liquid as possible.

2. Preheat the air fryer to 400°F.

3. Place the vegetable mixture back in the bowl and add the scallions, egg, breadcrumbs, Parmesan, and dill. Mix gently until thoroughly combined. Divide the mixture into 8 equal portions and shape into patties.

4. Arrange the patties in the air fryer basket, making sure they don't touch. Spritz with olive oil. Working in batches if necessary, air fry for 3 minutes, then remove and carefully flip. Air fry for an additional 3 to 4 minutes or until golden.

5. Garnish with fresh dill and serve with the sour cream on the side.

TIP: Allowing the salted vegetables to sit for a few minutes makes it far easier to extract as much water as you can, which will result in firmer patties.

Per serving: 245 calories, 9 g protein, 31 g carbohydrates, 8 g fat (4.5 g sat fat), 3 g fiber

Perfect Steak Fries

Makes 4 servings • Prep time: 5 minutes • Total time: 20 minutes

2 large russet potatoes, scrubbed and cut into wedges

1 tablespoon olive oil

1 teaspoon kosher salt

½ teaspoon freshly ground black pepper

Chopped fresh thyme, for garnish (optional)

Once you've tasted fries from your air fryer, you'll be hooked! The hot circulating air of the air fryer really helps seal in the flavor of the potato, but the key to crispy success is avoiding an overcrowded basket. Depending on the size of your air fryer, work in batches if necessary.

1. Preheat the air fryer to 400°F.

2. In a large bowl, combine the potatoes, oil, salt, and pepper. Toss until thoroughly coated.

3. Transfer the wedges to the air fryer basket. Air fry for 15 minutes, pausing every 5 minutes to shake the basket, until the fries are golden and crispy.

4. Serve garnished with thyme (if using).

Per serving: 175 calories, 4 g protein, 32 g carbohydrates, 4 g fat (0.5 g sat fat), 3 g fiber

Sweet Onion Rings

Makes 4 servings • Prep time: 15 minutes • Total time: 22 minutes + soaking time

1 large Vidalia onion, sliced into ⅛-inch rounds (about 20 rings)

½ cup all-purpose flour

½ teaspoon salt, plus additional for seasoning

½ teaspoon baking powder

½ teaspoon freshly ground black pepper

2 large eggs, beaten

1 cup panko breadcrumbs

Don't think of onion rings as part of a healthy weight loss eating plan? The truth is, your air fryer makes treats like these guilt-free! These skinnier rings will not only add significantly less fat to your diet than traditional deep-fried rings, but they're easy to make, too.

1. Soak the onion slices in ice water for 30 minutes to firm them up and seal in their flavor. Drain in a colander.

2. Preheat the air fryer to 400°F.

3. In a shallow bowl, stir together the flour, salt, baking powder, and pepper until combined. Place the eggs and breadcrumbs in separate shallow bowls. Dredge each of the onion rings in the flour mixture, followed by the eggs, and finally the breadcrumbs. Shake off any excess coating and spritz lightly with olive oil.

4. Arrange the onion rings in the air fryer basket, making sure they don't touch. Working in batches if necessary, air fry for 7 minutes, pausing halfway through the cooking time to turn the rings, or until they're golden.

5. Season with additional salt to taste before serving.

Per serving: 175 calories, 3 g protein, 35 g carbohydrates, 1 g fat (0 g sat fat), 1 g fiber

Guilt-Free Veggie Egg Rolls

Makes 4 servings • Prep time: 15 minutes • Total time: 23 minutes

2 cups shredded coleslaw mix

4 scallions, thinly sliced

2 tablespoons sesame seeds

1 tablespoon reduced-sodium soy sauce

1 tablespoon grated fresh ginger

8 egg roll wrappers

1 tablespoon toasted sesame oil

¼ cup sweet chili sauce, for dipping

Using shredded coleslaw mix is a great shortcut for getting these homemade egg rolls into your air fryer even faster. If you have time, assemble an extra batch to tuck into your freezer. Simply add a few minutes to your cooking time and they can go straight from the freezer into the air fryer.

1. In a large bowl, stir together the coleslaw mix, scallions, sesame seeds, soy sauce, and ginger until thoroughly combined.

2. To assemble the egg rolls, place a wrapper on a clean, dry surface with one corner facing you. Spoon about ¼ cup of the coleslaw mixture evenly onto the wrapper near the bottom corner. Lift this corner up and roll tightly to the middle of the wrapper. Fold the sides in, then continue rolling, tucking in the edges in as you go. Dab a small amount of water onto the remaining corner with your fingertip, then press it against the egg roll to seal. Repeat with the remaining wrappers and filling.

3. Brush the egg rolls with the sesame oil and place them in the basket seam-side down, leaving space between them. Air fry at 375°F for 5 to 8 minutes or until golden and crunchy.

4. Serve with the sweet chili sauce on the side.

Per serving (2 eggrolls): 300 calories, 0 g protein, 48 g carbohydrates, 7 g fat (1 g sat fat), 4 g fiber

Crab Rangoon

Makes 6 servings • Prep time: 15 minutes • Total time: 35 minutes

8 ounces Neufchâtel cheese, at room temperature

4 ounces lump crabmeat, drained

2 tablespoons minced scallion

1 tablespoon reduced-sodium soy sauce

30 square wonton wrappers

¾ cup sweet chili sauce, for dipping

If weight loss is your goal, ingredients matter. Neufchâtel, for example, has about 30 percent less fat than regular cream cheese. However, cooking methods make a big difference, too, and in this case your air fryer is saving you about 16 grams of fat per serving compared to a deep-fried version.

1. Preheat the air fryer to 350°F.

2. In a bowl, combine the Neufchâtel, crabmeat, scallion, and soy sauce and mix until thoroughly combined.

3. Working with one wrapper at a time, place a teaspoon of filling in the center of the wonton. Use your finger to moisten the edges of the wonton with warm water to form a sticky surface, and then lift the opposite corners up to meet in the center, pressing gently to seal. Seal the edges of the dumpling, pressing out as much air as you can.

4. Arrange the dumplings in the air fryer basket so they don't touch and spritz lightly with olive oil. Air fry for 6 minutes until crisp and golden.

5. Serve with the sweet chili sauce on the side.

Per serving: 300 calories, 11 g protein, 42 g carbohydrates, 9 g fat (5 g sat fat), 2 g fiber

Bacon-Wrapped Asparagus

Makes 4 servings • Prep time: 10 minutes • Total time: 20 minutes

8 slices reduced-sodium bacon, cut in half

16 thick asparagus spears (about 1 pound), trimmed of woody ends

1 lemon, cut into wedges

There are few foods that don't taste better wrapped in bacon, and asparagus is hardly the exception. An added bonus: the circulating heat of your air fryer ensures that each piece is evenly browned.

1. Preheat the air fryer to 350°F.

2. Wrap a half piece of bacon around the center of each stalk of asparagus.

3. Working in batches, if necessary, arrange seam-side down in a single layer in the air fryer basket. Air fry for 10 minutes until the bacon is crisp and the stalks are tender.

4. Serve with lemon wedges.

TIP: If large asparagus spears aren't available, wrap each piece of bacon around two or three thinner spears.

Per serving: 130 calories, 10 g protein, 5 g carbohydrates, 9 g fat (2.5 g sat fat), 2 g fiber

Smoky Chickpeas

Makes 4 servings • Prep time: 5 minutes • Total time: 25 minutes

1 (15-ounce) can chickpeas, rinsed and drained

1 tablespoon olive oil

2 teaspoons fresh lime juice

½ teaspoon salt

½ teaspoon smoked paprika

½ teaspoon garlic powder

Be forewarned—these crispy chickpeas are addictive! But you can feel good knowing that they're packed with protein and fiber. Enjoy them on their own, as a topping for salads, or a great crunchy addition to a wrap or sandwich.

1. Preheat the air fryer to 380°F.

2. Place the chickpeas in the air fryer basket and air fry for 15 minutes, pausing a few times to shake the basket, until the chickpeas are dry and beginning to crisp.

3. Meanwhile, in a large bowl, stir together the olive oil, lime juice, salt, paprika, and garlic powder until combined. Carefully transfer the chickpeas to the bowl and use a silicone spatula to stir until the chickpeas are thoroughly coated.

4. Return the seasoned chickpeas to the air fryer basket and reduce the temperature to 350°F. Air fry for 2 to 3 minutes longer until crisp.

5. The chickpeas will become crunchy as they cool. Serve at room temperature. Store in an airtight container for 3 to 5 days.

TIP: Cooking the chickpeas first until they dry ensures the seasonings remain flavorful.

Per serving: 160 calories, 7 g protein, 22 g carbohydrates, 6 g fat (1 g sat fat), 6 g fiber

Crispy Tofu Bites

Makes 4 servings • Prep time: 5 minutes • Total time: 20 minutes

1 pound extra-firm tofu, drained and pressed

1 tablespoon olive oil

2 teaspoons dry rub barbecue seasoning

½ teaspoon salt

½ cup barbecue sauce

The key to great-tasting tofu is to make sure you press as much liquid out of it as possible before cooking so that it absorbs flavors well. In this super-simple recipe, you can season the tofu right on your cutting board and massage it gently with your hands before transferring it to your air fryer. Serve with pickled cucumber slices.

1. Preheat the air fryer to 380°F.

2. Slice the tofu into 1-inch cubes, drizzle with the olive oil, and sprinkle with the barbecue seasoning and salt. Toss gently with your hands until the cubes are completely coated.

3. Arrange the tofu in a single layer in your air fryer basket. Air fry for 10 to 15 minutes, pausing every 5 minutes to shake the basket, until the tofu begins to brown and crisp at the edges.

4. Carefully transfer the tofu to a large bowl and top with the barbecue sauce. Use a silicone spatula to toss gently until thoroughly coated.

Per serving: 200 calories, 11 g protein, 18 g carbohydrates, 9 g fat (1.2 g sat fat), 2 g fiber

weeknight dinners

California-Style Turkey Burgers 46

Thai Chicken Skewers
with Peanut Sauce 49

Tandoori Chicken
with Cucumber Raita 50

Caribbean Chicken
with Mango Salsa 51

Chicken Fajitas 52

General Tso's Chicken 54

Chinese Chicken Patties 55

Chicken Cobb Salad
with Buffalo Drizzle 57

Asian Pork Salad 58

Easy Weeknight Pork Kebabs 61

Chicken Parmigiana 62

Favorite Lemon Chicken 63

Simply Terrific Turkey Meatballs 64

Greek Meatballs
with Tzatziki Sauce 67

Pork Tenderloin
with Apricot Glaze 68

Cuban Tenderloin 69

Garlic Rosemary Pork Chops
with Roasted Asparagus 70

Ham and Cheese Calzones 73

Korean Beef in Lettuce Cups 74

Stuffed Peppers 75

Homestyle Meatloaf 76

Breaded Chicken Tenders with
Maple-Mustard Dipping Sauce 78

New Classic Fish Sticks 79

Spicy Roasted Shrimp 81

Better-Than-Takeout
Shrimp and Broccoli 82

Barbecue-Glazed Salmon 83

Miso-Glazed Cod 84

Lemon-Pepper Tilapia 87

Fish Tacos with Quick-Pickled Onions
and Peppers 88

Stacked Black Bean Enchiladas 90

Vegetarian Shepherd's Pie 91

Cauliflower "Steaks"
with Chimichurri Sauce 93

Portobello Pizzas 94

California-Style Turkey Burgers

Makes 4 servings • Prep time: 10 minutes • Total time: 25 minutes

1 pound 93% lean ground turkey

1 tablespoon Dijon mustard

1 tablespoon reduced-fat mayonnaise

Salt and freshly ground black pepper

4 hamburger buns with sesame seeds

4 slices low-fat Monterey Jack cheese

½ cup shredded carrot

½ cup baby spinach

1 tomato, thinly sliced

You may never have considered shredded carrots to be an essential sandwich ingredient, but it's an easy way to add a sweet little crunch to your burgers. And there's no need for added condiments when mustard and mayonnaise are already incorporated into the patties to keep them juicy in the air fryer.

1. Preheat the air fryer to 360°F.

2. In a large bowl, stir together the turkey, Dijon, and mayonnaise. Season with salt and pepper. Mix until thoroughly combined, then divide the mixture and shape into 4 patties.

3. Arrange the patties in the air fryer basket so they are not touching. Air fry for 15 minutes, pausing halfway through the cooking time to flip the burgers, until browned and the temperature in the thickest portion is 165°F.

4. Place the patties on the buns and top with the cheese, carrot, spinach, and tomato slices before serving.

Per serving: 380 calories, 33 g protein, 22 g carbohydrates, 19 g fat (7 g sat fat), 4 g fiber

Thai Chicken Skewers with Peanut Sauce

Makes 4 servings • Prep time: 15 minutes • Total time: 25 minutes + marinating time

CHICKEN SKEWERS

2 tablespoons Thai red curry paste

2 tablespoons canola oil

1 tablespoon fresh lime juice

2 cloves garlic, minced

1½ pounds chicken tenders

PEANUT SAUCE

⅓ cup creamy peanut butter

Juice of ½ lime

1 tablespoon reduced-sodium soy sauce

1 teaspoon brown sugar

1 teaspoon grated fresh ginger

1 teaspoon chili-garlic sauce

¼ cup water

There are so many ways to enjoy this chicken dish! Serve the seasoned chicken with brown rice, noodles, or cucumber salad, or load it into a whole-grain wrap with your favorite crisp veggies.

1. To make the chicken skewers: In a small bowl, whisk together the curry paste, oil, lime juice, and garlic until smooth. Transfer the mixture to a large resealable bag. Add the chicken, seal the bag, and massage the bag to ensure the chicken is evenly coated. Refrigerate for 1 hour (or up to 8 hours).

2. To make the peanut sauce: In a medium bowl, whisk together the peanut butter, lime juice, soy sauce, brown sugar, ginger, and chili-garlic sauce until combined. Slowly add the water and whisk until smooth. Cover and refrigerate until ready to use.

3. To finish the dish, preheat the air fryer to 400°F.

4. Discard the marinade and thread the chicken back and forth onto metal skewers that fit in your air fryer. Working in batches if necessary, air fry the skewers for 10 to 12 minutes until cooked through, pausing halfway through the time to turn the skewers and lightly baste with a few tablespoons of the peanut sauce.

5. Serve with the remaining peanut sauce for dipping.

TIP: Covered and refrigerated, the peanut sauce will easily keep for up to a week.

Per serving: 410 calories, 45 g protein, 8 g carbohydrates, 23 g fat (4 g sat fat), 1 g fiber

Tandoori Chicken with Cucumber Raita

Makes 4 servings • Prep time: 10 minutes • Total time: 25 minutes + marinating time

1 cup plain nonfat Greek yogurt, divided

2 cloves garlic, minced

1 tablespoon grated fresh ginger

½ teaspoon ground cayenne

½ teaspoon ground turmeric

½ teaspoon garam masala

1 teaspoon ground cumin

1 teaspoon salt

1½ pounds boneless, skinless chicken breasts

1 small cucumber, peeled and shredded

1 small carrot, peeled and shredded

1 lemon, cut into 6 wedges, divided

2 tablespoons chopped fresh mint

2 tablespoons chopped fresh cilantro

½ sweet onion, sliced

A tandoor is a traditional clay oven that cooks food quickly at very high heat and is used throughout many parts of the Middle East and Asia. While your air fryer won't be able to match those temperatures, the convenience it affords is the next best thing. Serve with brown basmati rice.

1. In a small bowl, whisk ¼ cup of the yogurt with the garlic, ginger, cayenne, turmeric, garam masala, cumin, and salt until smooth.

2. Transfer the yogurt mixture to a large resealable bag. Add the chicken, seal the bag, and massage the bag to ensure the chicken is evenly coated. Refrigerate for 1 hour (or up to 8 hours).

3. Preheat the air fryer to 360°F.

4. Remove the chicken from the marinade (discard the marinade) and arrange in a single layer in the air fryer basket. Air fry for 15 to 20 minutes, pausing halfway through the cooking time to flip the chicken, until a meat thermometer inserted into the thickest part reaches 165°F.

5. Meanwhile, prepare the raita. In a bowl, combine the remaining ¾ cup yogurt with the cucumber, carrot, juice of 2 lemon wedges, and mint. Season to taste with salt.

6. Garnish the chicken with the cilantro. Serve the chicken alongside the raita, remaining 4 lemon wedges, and sliced onion.

Per serving: *240 calories, 45 g protein, 5 g carbohydrates, 4 g fat (1.3 g sat fat), 1 g fiber*

Caribbean Chicken with Mango Salsa

Makes 4 servings • Prep time: 15 minutes • Total time: 30 minutes

CARIBBEAN CHICKEN

2 tablespoons brown sugar

1 tablespoon ground allspice

1 teaspoon salt

1 teaspoon cumin

1 teaspoon dried thyme

½ teaspoon cayenne pepper (optional)

1½ pounds boneless, skinless chicken breasts

1 tablespoon olive oil

MANGO SALSA

1 large mango, peeled and diced (about 2 cups)

¼ red bell pepper, seeded and finely diced

2 scallions, finely chopped

Juice of ½ lime

2 tablespoons chopped fresh cilantro

¼ teaspoon salt

If you have the time, prep these spice-rubbed chicken breasts and pop them into a resealable bag in your fridge overnight. The flavors will only improve. However, if time is tight, this spice rub can work magic in the air fryer without that extra step.

1. Preheat the air fryer to 360°F.

2. To make the chicken: In a small bowl, stir together the brown sugar, allspice, salt, cumin, thyme, and cayenne (if using) until combined. Rub the chicken breasts with the spice mixture until thoroughly coated and then drizzle with the olive oil.

3. Arrange the chicken in a single layer in the air fryer basket. Air fry for 15 to 20 minutes, pausing halfway through the cooking time to flip the chicken, until a meat thermometer inserted into the thickest part reaches 165°F.

4. Meanwhile, to make the mango salsa: In a large bowl, combine the mango, bell pepper, scallions, lime juice, cilantro, and salt.

5. Serve the chicken topped with the mango salsa.

Per serving: 305 calories, 40 g protein, 21 g carbohydrates, 8 g fat (1.8 g sat fat), 2 g fiber

Chicken Fajitas

Makes 4 servings • Prep time: 15 minutes • Total time: 30 minutes

1 pound chicken breast tenders, chopped into bite-size pieces

½ onion, thinly sliced

½ red bell pepper, seeded and thinly sliced

½ green bell pepper, seeded and thinly sliced

1 tablespoon vegetable oil

1 tablespoon fajita seasoning

1 teaspoon kosher salt

Juice of ½ lime

8 small flour tortillas

½ cup prepared guacamole

It's time to reimagine family taco night! You don't need beef, cheese, and fried taco shells to create a fiesta when your air fryer can help you get an alternative dish on the table quickly. These easy chicken fajitas are every bit as delicious and far easier to fit into a healthy weight loss plan.

1. Preheat the air fryer to 400°F.

2. In a large bowl, combine the chicken, onion, and peppers. Drizzle with the vegetable oil and toss until thoroughly coated. Add the fajita seasoning and salt and toss again.

3. Working in batches if necessary, arrange the chicken and vegetables in a single layer in the air fryer basket. Air fry for 15 minutes, pausing halfway through the cooking time to shake the basket, until the vegetables are tender and the chicken is cooked through.

4. Transfer the mixture to a serving platter and drizzle with the fresh lime juice.

5. Place the chicken mixture on the tortillas and serve with the guacamole.

Per serving: 410 calories, 32 g protein, 37 g carbohydrates, 15 g fat (3.1 g sat fat), 5 g fiber

General Tso's Chicken

Makes 4 servings • Prep time: 10 minutes • Total time: 25 minutes

4 boneless, skinless chicken thighs (about 1¼ pounds)

Salt and freshly ground black pepper

2 tablespoons cornstarch

2 tablespoons rice vinegar

2 tablespoons reduced-sodium soy sauce

2 teaspoons hoisin sauce

2 tablespoons sugar

2 cloves garlic, minced

1 teaspoon sriracha (optional)

2 scallions, thinly sliced

1 tablespoon sesame seeds

While you'll never find this dish if you happen to travel to China, its popularity as a Chinese-American staple is well deserved. Most deep-fried versions rely on cornstarch to help make the chicken extra crispy. Fortunately, with an air fryer you can get similar results but skip the added fat and calories.

1. Preheat the air fryer to 400°F.

2. Cut the chicken into bite-size pieces and place in a large bowl. Season with salt and pepper. Sprinkle with the cornstarch and toss to coat.

3. Spread the chicken in the air fryer basket in a single layer and spritz lightly with olive oil. Air fry for 15 minutes, pausing halfway through the cooking time to shake the basket, until the chicken is cooked through.

4. Meanwhile, in another large bowl, whisk together the vinegar, soy sauce, hoisin sauce, sugar, garlic, and sriracha (if using). Transfer the cooked chicken to the bowl and toss to coat.

5. Top with the scallions and sesame seeds before serving.

Per serving: 270 calories, 28 g protein, 17 g carbohydrates, 10 g fat (2.9 g sat fat), 1 g fiber

Chinese Chicken Patties

Makes 4 servings • Prep time: 10 minutes • Total time: 20 minutes

1½ pounds extra-lean ground chicken breast

1 (8-ounce) can water chestnuts, drained and chopped

3 tablespoons hoisin sauce

3 scallions, thinly sliced

1 tablespoon grated fresh ginger

These five-ingredient chicken patties are quick to put together and so very versatile. Serve with brown rice and steamed vegetables, or if you are watching your carb intake, try them in lettuce cups.

1. Preheat the air fryer to 400°F.

2. In a large bowl, stir together the chicken, water chestnuts, hoisin sauce, scallions, and ginger until thoroughly combined. Shape into 8 patties, each about ½ inch thick.

3. Arrange the patties in a single layer in the air fryer basket. Spritz lightly with olive oil. Air fry for 10 minutes, or until the temperature in the thickest portion of the patty registers 165°F.

Per serving: 240 calories, 36 g protein, 12 g carbohydrates, 6 g fat (1 g sat fat), 2 g fiber

Chicken Cobb Salad
with Buffalo Drizzle

Makes 4 servings • Prep time: 20 minutes • Total time: 35 minutes

2 boneless, skinless chicken breasts (about 1 pound)

Salt and freshly ground black pepper

2 tablespoons unsalted butter

2 tablespoons hot sauce

2 tablespoons olive oil

2 teaspoons cider vinegar

8 cups chopped romaine

2 hard-boiled eggs, chopped

¼ cup crumbled blue cheese

1 cup cherry tomatoes, chopped

¼ cup chopped red onion

1 avocado, halved, pitted, and chopped

Spice up a classic combination of Cobb salad fixings with a rich drizzle of buttery hot sauce! If you're a big Buffalo wing fan, this zesty chicken salad is sure to please your taste buds while helping you stay on track with smart eating.

1. Preheat the air fryer to 380°F.

2. Season the chicken breasts with salt and pepper. Spritz lightly with olive oil spray. Arrange the chicken in a single layer in the air fryer basket. Air fry for 15 to 20 minutes, pausing halfway through the cooking time to flip the chicken, until a meat thermometer inserted into the thickest part reaches 165°F.

3. Meanwhile, in a large microwave-safe bowl, melt the butter in the microwave on high for 1 minute. Whisk in the hot sauce and set aside.

4. In another large bowl, whisk together the olive oil and vinegar until thoroughly combined. Season to taste with salt and pepper. Add the romaine and toss to coat. Arrange the eggs, blue cheese, tomatoes, red onion, and avocado on top.

5. When the chicken is cool enough to handle, slice into thin pieces or chop into bite-size pieces and add to the butter mixture. Toss until the chicken is thoroughly coated. Top the salad with the chicken and drizzle any sauce that remains on top.

Per serving: *395 calories, 33 g protein, 7 g carbohydrates, 26 g fat (8.2 g sat fat), 4 g fiber*

Asian Pork Salad

Makes 4 servings • Prep time: 20 minutes • Total time: 30 minutes + marinating time

Juice of 1 lime

2 tablespoons reduced-sodium soy sauce

1 tablespoon fish sauce

2 tablespoons toasted sesame oil, divided

1 tablespoon minced lemongrass paste (optional)

1 pound boneless pork roast, trimmed and thinly sliced

1 (8.8 ounce) package vermicelli rice noodles

½ sweet onion, thinly sliced

2 scallions. chopped

2 carrots, shredded

1 cucumber, julienned

4 cups chopped romaine

Salt

4 small sprigs fresh mint

¼ cup prepared fried shallots (optional)

If you love Asian food, keep this satisfying salad in your regular dinner rotation for its speed and convenience. Once the pork has marinated, this dish only requires about 10 minutes in the air fryer, which is plenty of time to cook the noodles and prep the rest of the vegetables.

1. In a large bowl, whisk together the lime juice, soy sauce, fish sauce, 1 tablespoon of the sesame oil, and lemongrass paste (if using). Add the pork and toss until thoroughly coated. Let sit at room temperature for 30 minutes or cover and refrigerate overnight.

2. Preheat the air fryer to 400°F.

3. Spread the pork in a single layer in the air fryer basket. Air fry for 10 minutes, pausing halfway through the cooking time to turn the meat, until cooked through and the edges begin to crisp.

4. Meanwhile, prepare the vermicelli according to the package instructions and rinse the noodles under cold water to stop the cooking process. Transfer the noodles to another large bowl and toss with the remaining 1 tablespoon of sesame oil.

5. Arrange the noodles, onion, scallions, carrot, cucumber, and romaine in bowls. Season to taste with salt. Serve topped with the pork, fresh mint, and shallots (if using).

Per serving: 535 calories, 37 g protein, 53 g carbohydrates, 19 g fat (5 g sat fat), 2 g fiber

Easy Weeknight Pork Kebabs

Makes 4 servings • Prep time: 15 minutes • Total time: 25 minutes

¼ cup orange juice

2 tablespoons honey

2 tablespoons Worcestershire sauce

1 tablespoon olive oil

1 large clove garlic, minced

2 bell peppers, preferably red or orange

1 pork tenderloin (about 1¼ pounds)

Trimming a pork tenderloin into small bite-size cubes means it will cook even faster in your air fryer, and sandwiching chunks of bell pepper in between the meat helps all the flavors combine as the kebabs roast. Feel free to add some onions or zucchini to the mix if you prefer, but this simple combination helps you save time with delicious results.

1. In a large bowl, whisk together the orange juice, honey, Worcestershire sauce, olive oil, and garlic.

2. Cut the tops off the peppers, remove the seeds, and cut each pepper into 8 equal pieces. Slice the pork into 16 equal pieces. Transfer the peppers and pork to the bowl with the marinade mixture and toss until thoroughly coated.

3. Preheat the air fryer to 400°F.

4. Thread the pork and peppers onto 4 metal skewers that will fit inside the air fryer basket. Arrange the kebabs in the air fryer basket so they are not touching and air fry for 10 to 12 minutes, pausing halfway through the cooking time to flip the kebabs, until a meat thermometer inserted into the thickest portion reaches 145°F.

Per serving: 250 calories, 31 g protein, 16 g carbohydrates, 7 g fat (1.5 g sat fat), 1 g fiber

Chicken Parmigiana

Makes 4 servings • Prep time: 10 minutes • Total time: 28 minutes

2 large boneless, skinless chicken breasts (about 1¼ pounds)

Salt and freshly ground black pepper

1 cup panko breadcrumbs

½ cup grated Parmesan cheese

2 teaspoons Italian seasoning

1 large egg, lightly beaten

1 cup marinara sauce

2 ounces fresh mozzarella, sliced

2 tablespoons chopped fresh basil

What started as a riff on a traditional way to serve eggplant has become an Italian-American favorite. Fortunately, you don't have to forego this beloved and tasty classic when you have an air fryer to help you slash unnecessary calories from the finished dish.

1. Preheat the air fryer to 360°F.

2. Slice the chicken breasts in half horizontally to create 4 thinner chicken breasts. Working with one piece at a time, place the chicken between two pieces of parchment paper and pound with a meat mallet or rolling pin to flatten to an even thickness. Season both sides with salt and pepper.

3. In a large shallow bowl, stir together the breadcrumbs, Parmesan, and Italian seasoning until thoroughly combined. Place the egg in another large shallow bowl. Dip the chicken in the egg, followed by the breadcrumb mixture, pressing firmly to create an even coating.

4. Working in batches if necessary, arrange the chicken breasts in a single layer in the air fryer basket and coat both sides lightly with vegetable oil. Pausing halfway through the cooking time to flip the chicken, air fry for 15 minutes, or until a meat thermometer inserted into the thickest part reaches 165°F.

5. Spoon the marinara sauce over each piece of chicken and top with the mozzarella cheese. Air fry for an additional 3 to 5 minutes until the cheese is melted.

6. Garnish with the basil before serving.

Per serving: 410 calories, 44 g protein, 28 g carbohydrates, 9 g fat (4.9 g sat fat), 2 g fiber

Favorite Lemon Chicken

Makes 4 servings • Prep time: 10 minutes • Total time: 30 minutes

4 boneless, skinless chicken breasts (about 1½ pounds)

1 tablespoon olive oil

1½ teaspoons lemon-pepper seasoning

½ teaspoon paprika

½ teaspoon garlic powder

¼ teaspoon dried oregano

¼ teaspoon freshly ground black pepper

Juice of ½ lemon

To save time later in the week, prepare a double batch of this chicken. It will surely get gobbled up! Leftover cooked chicken breast is a great source of lean protein and a lifesaver for tossing into pasta dishes, on top of salads, or in sandwiches or wraps.

1. Preheat the air fryer to 360°F.

2. Place the chicken in a large bowl and drizzle with the olive oil. Top with the lemon-pepper seasoning, paprika, garlic powder, oregano, and pepper. Toss until thoroughly coated.

3. Working in batches if necessary, arrange the chicken in a single layer in the air fryer basket. Air fry for 20 to 25 minutes, pausing halfway through the cooking time to turn the chicken, until a meat thermometer inserted into the thickest piece reaches 165°F.

4. Transfer the chicken to a serving platter and squeeze the lemon juice over the top.

Per serving: 225 calories, 39 g protein, 0 g carbohydrates, 7 g fat (1.7 g sat fat), 0 g fiber

Simply Terrific Turkey Meatballs

Makes 4 servings • Prep time: 10 minutes • Total time: 20 minutes

¼ sweet onion

2 cloves garlic, coarsely chopped

¼ cup coarsely chopped fresh parsley

1 pound 85% lean ground turkey

1 large egg, lightly beaten

¾ cup panko breadcrumbs

1 teaspoon salt

½ teaspoon freshly ground black pepper

Finely chopped onion, garlic, and parsley add both moisture and flavor to these juicy meatballs. Pair them with pasta and marinara or load them into a meatball sandwich. However you serve them, they'll be a hit every time!

1. Preheat the air fryer to 400°F.

2. In a food processor fitted with a metal blade, pulse the onion, garlic, and parsley until finely chopped. Transfer the vegetables to a large mixing bowl.

3. Add the turkey, egg, breadcrumbs, salt, and pepper. Mix gently until thoroughly combined. Shape the mixture into 1¼-inch meatballs.

4. Working in batches if necessary, arrange the meatballs in a single layer in the air fryer basket; spritz lightly with olive oil. Air fry for 7 to 10 minutes, pausing halfway through the cooking time to shake the basket, until lightly browned and a meat thermometer inserted into the center of a meatball reaches 165°F.

Per serving: 300 calories, 23 g protein, 16 g carbohydrates, 14 g fat (3.5 g sat fat), 0 g fiber

Greek Meatballs with Tzatziki Sauce

Makes 4 servings • Prep time: 10 minutes • Total time: 20 minutes

GREEK MEATBALLS

1 pound extra-lean ground chicken

1 large egg

4 cloves garlic, grated

2 teaspoons dried oregano

1 teaspoon dried thyme

1 teaspoon lemon zest

Salt and freshly ground black pepper

TZATZIKI SAUCE

1 cup nonfat Greek yogurt

½ cucumber, grated

1 tablespoon fresh lemon juice

1 clove garlic, grated

½ teaspoon salt

4 (6-inch) pitas

Fresh lettuce, for garnish

When you're hankering for a juicy gyro, let your kitchen tools save the day. Your air fryer will slash calories and fat without sacrificing flavor. A Microplane grater, the same tool you use to grate the lemon zest, ensures garlicky goodness with every bite.

1. Preheat the air fryer to 400°F.

2. To make the meatballs: In a large bowl, stir together the chicken, egg, garlic, oregano, thyme, and lemon zest. Season with salt and pepper. Mix gently until thoroughly combined. Shape the mixture into 1¼-inch meatballs.

3. Working in batches if necessary, arrange the meatballs in a single layer in the air fryer basket; spritz lightly with olive oil. Air fry for 7 to 10 minutes, pausing halfway through the cooking time to shake the basket, until lightly browned and a meat thermometer inserted into the center of a meatball reaches 165°F.

4. To make the tzatziki sauce: Stir together the yogurt, cucumber, lemon juice, garlic, and salt in a small bowl until thoroughly combined.

5. Serve the meatballs with the lettuce in the pita bread and top with the tzatziki sauce.

Per serving: *345 calories, 37 g protein, 38 g carbohydrates, 5 g fat (0.8 g sat fat), 2 g fiber*

Pork Tenderloin with Apricot Glaze

Makes 4 servings • Prep time: 10 minutes • Total time: 28 minutes

⅓ cup apricot preserves

1 tablespoon Dijon mustard

1 pork tenderloin (about 1 pound)

2 teaspoons olive oil

½ teaspoon dried thyme

½ teaspoon salt

¼ teaspoon freshly ground black pepper

Lean pork tenderloin pairs so perfectly with a sweet apricot glaze! And with 24 grams of protein for only 205 calories, this dish is sure to become one of your air fryer favorites.

1. Preheat the air fryer to 360°F.

2. In a small bowl, stir together the preserves and Dijon and mix until thoroughly combined. Set aside.

3. Rub the pork with the olive oil, thyme, salt, and pepper. Arrange the pork in the air fryer basket. Air fry for 18 to 20 minutes, pausing halfway through the cooking time to turn the pork and brush with half the glaze, until a meat thermometer inserted into the thickest portion reaches 145°F. Brush again with the remaining glaze 2 to 3 minutes before the pork is done.

4. Let the pork rest for 5 minutes before slicing.

TIP: If necessary, cut the tenderloin into two pieces so that it fits easily in your air fryer basket.

Per serving: 205 calories, 24 g protein, 16 g carbohydrates, 5 g fat (1.1 g sat fat), 0 g fiber

Cuban Tenderloin

Makes 4 servings • Prep time: 10 minutes • Total time: 30 minutes + marinating time

1 pork tenderloin (about 1 pound)

½ cup orange juice

Juice of 1 lime

1 tablespoon olive oil

2 teaspoons ground cumin

6 cloves garlic, chopped

½ teaspoon salt

¼ teaspoon freshly ground black pepper

¼ cup chopped fresh cilantro

Once you account for the marinating time, this dish goes from the air fryer to the table with incredible ease. To boost your fiber intake, serve with a side of black beans and brown rice. And if you are lucky enough to have leftovers, they're a perfect main ingredient for a Cuban sandwich; just add some deli ham, mustard, Swiss cheese, and pickles.

1. In a large resealable bag, combine the pork, orange juice, lime juice, olive oil, cumin, garlic, salt, and pepper. Massage lightly to coat the pork. Refrigerate for 4 hours or overnight.

2. Preheat the air fryer to 360°F.

3. Remove the pork from the marinade and discard the marinade. Arrange the pork in the air fryer basket and spritz lightly with olive oil. Air fry for 18 to 20 minutes, pausing halfway through the cooking time to turn the pork, until a meat thermometer inserted into the thickest portion reaches 145°F.

4. Let the pork rest for 5 minutes before slicing. Serve topped with the cilantro.

Per serving: 140 calories, 24 g protein, 2 g carbohydrates, 4 g fat (1 g sat fat), 0 g fiber

Garlic Rosemary Pork Chops with Roasted Asparagus

Makes 2 servings • Prep time: 10 minutes • Total time: 20 minutes

8 ounces asparagus spears

Salt and freshly ground black pepper

2 bone-in pork chops (about 12 ounces)

1 teaspoon olive oil

2 cloves garlic, minced

1 teaspoon Italian seasoning

2 tablespoons pesto

2 rosemary sprigs, for garnish

This easy, low-carb version of a one-dish meal for your air fryer is sure to win rave reviews. It comes together quickly, so if you're serving more than two people, simply cook in batches.

1. Preheat the air fryer to 380°F.

2. Snap the ends off the asparagus. Spritz lightly with olive oil and season to taste with salt and pepper. Set aside.

3. Drizzle the pork chops with the olive oil and top with the garlic, Italian seasoning, salt, and pepper. Rub the pork chops until thoroughly coated with the seasonings, then arrange the chops in the air fryer basket so that they are not touching.

4. Cook for 10 to 12 minutes, pausing halfway through the cooking time to turn the pork chops and add the asparagus, until a meat thermometer inserted into the thickest portion of a chop reaches 145°F and the asparagus is tender. Let rest for 5 minutes.

5. Serve topped with the pesto and the rosemary.

Per serving: 250 calories, 25 g protein, 6 g carbohydrates, 15 g fat (3.3 g sat fat), 2 g fiber

Ham and Cheese Calzones

Makes 4 servings • Prep time: 10 minutes • Total time: 20 minutes

2 tablespoons all-purpose flour

12 ounces pizza dough, divided into 4 equal pieces

8 ounces deli ham

1 cup shredded part-skim mozzarella cheese

¼ cup finely chopped red onion

2 teaspoons olive oil, divided

1 cup marinara sauce

Most grocery stores sell balls of premade pizza dough either fresh or frozen, which makes these delicious calzones super easy to put together in an air fryer. You'll likely need a kitchen scale to measure out a smaller portion for this recipe, but the unused dough will keep well for several days in your refrigerator. Do not refreeze dough that has been thawed.

1. Preheat the air fryer to 360°F.

2. Lightly dust your work surface with the flour, then stretch each piece of pizza dough into a thin circle. Divide the ham, cheese, and red onion on one half of each circle of dough. Fold the opposite side over the top to form semicircles. Pinch the edges closed. Brush each calzone lightly with ½ teaspoon of olive oil.

3. Working in batches if necessary, arrange the calzones in the air fryer basket. Air fry for 10 minutes or until lightly browned.

4. Meanwhile, place the marinara sauce in a microwave-safe bowl and heat for 1 minute on high until warm. Serve with the calzones.

Per serving: 425 calories, 24 g protein, 49 g carbohydrates, 14 g fat (4.8 g sat fat), 3 g fiber

Korean Beef in Lettuce Cups

Makes 4 servings • Prep time: 20 minutes • Total time: 30 minutes + marinating time

2 tablespoons gochujang (Korean chile paste)

2 cloves garlic, minced

2 teaspoons grated fresh ginger

1 tablespoon toasted sesame oil

1 tablespoon reduced-sodium soy sauce

1 tablespoon sesame seeds

2 teaspoons sugar

½ teaspoon salt

1 pound thinly sliced sirloin, trimmed of visible fat

1 small red onion, thinly sliced

2 heads butter lettuce, leaves separated into "cups"

4 scallions, thinly sliced

1 cup kimchi

Traditional Korean bulgogi, a delicious Asian barbecue specialty, is usually made with beef rib eye. However, if weight loss is your goal, you can turn to a leaner cut, like sirloin, that will work nicely in the air fryer. Both gochujang and kimchi come in varying degrees of spiciness, so choose the heat level you prefer.

1. In a small bowl, whisk together the gochujang, garlic, ginger, sesame oil, soy sauce, sesame seeds, sugar, and salt. Place the beef and onions in a resealable bag along with the marinade and massage gently until thoroughly coated. Let sit at room temperature for 30 minutes or refrigerate for up to 24 hours.

2. Preheat the air fryer to 400°F.

3. Transfer the meat and onions to the air fryer basket, leaving behind as much of the marinade as possible and spreading the meat in an even layer. Discard the marinade. Air fry for 10 minutes, pausing halfway through the cooking time to turn the meat, until browned and cooked through.

4. To serve, divide the beef and onions among the lettuce cups and top with the scallions and kimchi.

Per serving: 280 calories, 29 g protein, 8 g carbohydrates, 14 g fat (4.6 g sat fat), 3 g fiber

Stuffed Peppers

Makes 4 servings • Prep time: 15 minutes • Total time: 47 minutes

1 pound 85% lean ground beef

½ yellow onion, chopped

4 bell peppers, tops and seeds removed

1 (8.5-ounce) pouch microwave-ready quinoa and brown rice

½ cup crushed tomatoes

2 tablespoons chopped fresh parsley

¾ teaspoon salt

¼ teaspoon freshly ground black pepper

1 cup reduced-fat shredded Cheddar cheese

A package of ready-to-heat quinoa and brown rice helps boost both the fiber and the protein in this dish while still meeting all the requirements of a tried-and-true family favorite. An added bonus is that you can take advantage of all the peppers available in late summer and enjoy real comfort food without turning on the oven.

1. Preheat the air fryer to 400°F.

2. Crumble the beef into a single layer in the air fryer basket. Scatter the onion on top. Air fry for 15 to 20 minutes until the beef is browned and cooked through.

3. Meanwhile, arrange the bell peppers in a microwave-safe dish and cover loosely with parchment paper or plastic wrap. Microwave on high for 2 to 3 minutes until the peppers begin to soften.

4. To assemble the peppers, carefully transfer the beef and onions to a large mixing bowl. Use the side of a spoon to break up any large pieces of beef. Drain the grease and wash the air fryer basket. Turn the air fryer down to 360°F.

5. To the beef mixture, add the quinoa and rice, tomatoes, parsley, salt, and pepper. Stir gently until thoroughly combined.

6. Divide the mixture among the peppers and arrange cut-side up in the air fryer basket. Air fry for 15 to 20 minutes until the peppers are soft. Top with the cheese and air fry for 1 to 2 minutes longer until melted.

Per serving: 445 calories, 33 g protein, 35 g carbohydrates, 19 g fat (8.1 g sat fat), 5 g fiber

Homestyle Meatloaf

Makes 4 servings • Prep time: 15 minutes • Total time: 1 hour

1 small onion, coarsely chopped

1 rib celery, coarsely chopped

2 cloves garlic

1 pound 85% lean ground beef

1 large egg, lightly beaten

½ cup panko breadcrumbs

2 tablespoons milk

1 teaspoon salt

½ teaspoon freshly ground black pepper

2 tablespoons ketchup

1 tablespoon brown sugar

Nothing says comfort food like meatloaf, and this one fits the bill with a rich, sweet glaze of ketchup baked into the crust. Because the air fryer circulates hot air while it cooks, your meatloaf will be done a little faster than if you were to bake it in a conventional oven.

1. Preheat the air fryer to 350°F. Lightly coat an 8-inch round pan with olive oil and set aside.

2. In a food processor fitted with a metal blade, pulse the onion, celery, and garlic until finely chopped. Transfer the vegetables to a large mixing bowl.

3. Add the beef, egg, breadcrumbs, milk, salt, and pepper. Mix gently until thoroughly combined. Transfer the mixture to the prepared pan and shape into a loaf.

4. In a small bowl, stir together the ketchup and brown sugar. Pour the glaze over the meatloaf and spread evenly with the back of a spoon.

5. Air fry for 45 minutes or until the meatloaf is nicely browned and a meat thermometer inserted into the thickest part reaches 160°F. Remove from the air fryer and let rest for about 10 minutes before slicing.

Per serving: *295 calories, 22 g protein, 18 g carbohydrates, 13 g fat (5 g sat fat), 0 g fiber*

Breaded Chicken Tenders with Maple-Mustard Dipping Sauce

Makes 4 servings • Prep time: 20 minutes • Total time: 30 minutes + marinating

CHICKEN TENDERS

1½ pounds chicken breast tenders

1 cup buttermilk

1 teaspoon garlic powder

1 teaspoon salt

½ teaspoon freshly ground black pepper

½ teaspoon dried thyme

1 cup panko breadcrumbs

2 teaspoons Old Bay seasoning

MAPLE-MUSTARD SAUCE

¼ cup light pancake syrup

¼ cup Dijon mustard

Marinating not only infuses flavor but also ensures that a light coating of breadcrumbs will cling to the chicken breast tenders, resulting in a far healthier dish. Compared to traditionally deep-fried breaded chicken tenders, your air fryer saves you more than 10 grams of fat!

1. To make the chicken: In a large resealable bag, combine the chicken, buttermilk, garlic powder, salt, pepper, and thyme. Seal the bag and massage gently until the chicken is thoroughly coated. Refrigerate for at least 2 hours or overnight.

2. Preheat the air fryer to 400°F.

3. In a large bowl, stir together the breadcrumbs and Old Bay seasoning.

4. Remove the tenders from the marinade, letting most of the marinade drip off before transferring the chicken to the bowl with the breadcrumbs. Toss the tenders gently, pressing lightly to ensure an even coating.

5. Working in batches if necessary, arrange the tenders in a single layer in the air fryer basket and spritz lightly with olive oil. Air fry for 10 to 12 minutes, pausing halfway through the cooking time to turn the chicken, until cooked through.

6. To make the maple-mustard sauce: In a small bowl, stir together the syrup and Dijon until smooth. Serve with the chicken tenders for dipping.

Per serving: 375 calories, 42 g protein, 29 g carbohydrates, 7 g fat (1.7 g sat fat), 1 g fiber

New Classic Fish Sticks

Makes 4 servings • Prep time: 15 minutes • Total time: 30 minutes

FISH STICKS

1½ pounds cod fillets, cut into 1-inch strips

1 teaspoon salt

½ teaspoon freshly ground black pepper

¼ cup all-purpose flour

2 large eggs

1 cup panko breadcrumbs

TARTAR SAUCE

½ cup reduced-fat sour cream

½ cup reduced-fat mayonnaise

3 tablespoons chopped dill pickle

2 tablespoons capers, drained and chopped

½ teaspoon dried dill

1 tablespoon dill pickle liquid (optional)

If you're feeling nostalgic for a food flashback, try this new version of the classic family favorite. Thanks to the air fryer, you can enjoy great flavor with lightened fat and calories. It will taste far fresher than the sticks you buy in the freezer case!

1. Preheat the air fryer to 400°F.

2. To make the fish sticks: Season the cod with the salt and pepper and sprinkle with the flour, tossing until the fish is thoroughly coated; set aside.

3. In a shallow bowl, lightly beat the eggs. In a second shallow bowl, place the breadcrumbs.

4. Working with a few pieces at a time, dip the fish into the egg mixture followed by the breadcrumbs. Press lightly to ensure an even coating.

5. Working in batches if necessary, arrange the fish in a single layer in the air fryer basket and spritz lightly with olive oil. Air fry for 12 to 15 minutes, pausing halfway through the cooking time to turn the fish, until the fish flakes easily with a fork. Let sit in the basket for a few minutes before serving.

6. To make the tartar sauce: In a small bowl, whisk together the sour cream, mayonnaise, pickle, capers, and dill until thoroughly combined. If you prefer a thinner sauce, stir in the pickle liquid. Serve with the fish sticks.

Per serving: 450 calories, 35 g protein, 32 g carbohydrates, 17 g fat (4.3 g sat fat), 1 g fiber

Spicy Roasted Shrimp

Makes 4 servings • Prep time: 5 minutes • Total time: 20 minutes

2 tablespoons olive oil

3 cloves garlic, minced

Juice of 1 lemon

1 teaspoon salt

½ teaspoon freshly ground black pepper

½ teaspoon paprika

¼ teaspoon red pepper flakes (optional)

1½ pounds large uncooked shrimp, peeled and deveined

2 tablespoons chopped fresh cilantro

Tuck a bag of frozen shrimp in the back of your freezer and you'll always be prepared to make this super dish. To thaw shrimp quickly (and safely), simply submerge in a bowl of cold water for about 20 minutes. For best results, make sure to pat them dry with paper towels before proceeding with the recipe.

1. Preheat the air fryer to 370°F.

2. In a large bowl, stir together the olive oil, garlic, lemon juice, salt, pepper, paprika, and red pepper flakes (if using). Add the shrimp and toss until thoroughly coated.

3. Transfer the shrimp to the air fryer basket. Air fry for 12 to 15 minutes, pausing halfway through to shake the basket, until the shrimp are cooked through.

4. Top with the cilantro just before serving.

Per serving: 185 calories, 23 g protein, 3 g carbohydrates, 9 g fat (1.4 g sat fat), 0 g fiber

Better-Than-Takeout Shrimp and Broccoli

Makes 4 servings • Prep time: 10 minutes • Total time: 25 minutes

2 tablespoons reduced-sodium soy sauce

1 tablespoon sesame oil

2 teaspoons chile-garlic sauce

3 cloves garlic, minced

1 teaspoon grated fresh ginger

1½ pounds large uncooked shrimp, peeled and deveined

4 cups broccoli florets

¼ cup sesame seeds

Takeout can be tempting for convenience, but it often comes with a nutritional price. Why not enjoy the flavor of classic Chinese dishes while lightening up the fat and calorie load? Your air fryer makes it simple! And this dish can be ready in the same time it would take you to place an order and wait for delivery or pickup.

1. Preheat the air fryer to 370°F.

2. In a large bowl, stir together the soy sauce, sesame oil, chile-garlic sauce, garlic, and ginger. Add the shrimp and broccoli and toss until thoroughly coated.

3. Transfer the shrimp and broccoli to the air fryer basket. Air fry for 12 to 15 minutes, pausing halfway through the cooking time to shake the basket, until the shrimp are cooked through and the broccoli is tender.

4. Top with the sesame seeds just before serving.

Per serving: *245 calories, 28 g protein, 9 g carbohydrates, 11 g fat (1.8 g sat fat), 4 g fiber*

Barbecue-Glazed Salmon

Makes 4 servings • Prep time: 10 minutes • Total time: 18 minutes

½ cup barbecue sauce

2 tablespoons honey

1¼ pounds salmon fillets

½ teaspoon salt

2 scallions, thinly sliced

Lining the bottom of your air fryer with a piece of parchment will make cleanup a breeze. However, this is a recipe that requires careful attention. Glaze the salmon lightly at first because the extra sugar in the sauce will make it burn easily if it's in the air fryer too long.

1. Cut a piece of parchment to fit the bottom of the air fryer basket and set aside. Preheat the air fryer to 400°F.

2. In a small bowl, whisk together the barbecue sauce and honey.

3. Sprinkle the fish with the salt and brush lightly with the sauce. Arrange the fish on the parchment, skin-side down, so there is room between the pieces.

4. Air fry for 5 minutes, pausing to baste the fish again with the rest of the sauce. Continue air frying for 3 to 5 minutes longer until the fish is cooked through flakes easily with a fork.

5. Let sit for 5 minutes before serving. Top with the scallions.

Per serving: 365 calories, 29 g protein, 25 g carbohydrates, 16 g fat (3.2 g sat fat), 0 g fiber

Miso-Glazed Cod

Makes 4 servings • Prep time: 10 minutes • Total time: 18 minutes

1 tablespoon unsalted butter, melted

¼ cup white miso paste

2 tablespoons honey

1 tablespoon rice wine vinegar

½ teaspoon grated fresh ginger

1½ pounds cod

Salt and freshly ground black pepper

1 teaspoon toasted sesame oil

Miso, a classic Japanese condiment, is a fermented soybean paste that lends a deep flavor to an otherwise mild fish. However, Asian-inspired sides aren't essential. This dish pairs perfectly with a simple salad and boiled new potatoes.

1. Cut a piece of parchment to fit the bottom of the air fryer basket and set aside. Preheat the air fryer to 400°F.

2. In a small bowl, whisk together the butter, miso, honey, vinegar, and ginger until smooth.

3. Season the fish with the salt and pepper, then brush lightly with the oil followed by half of the sauce. Arrange the fish on the parchment so there is room between the pieces.

4. Air fry for 5 minutes, pausing to baste the fish again with the rest of the sauce. Continue air frying for 3 to 5 minutes longer until the fish is cooked through and flakes easily with a fork.

Per serving: 250 calories, 32 g protein, 15 g carbohydrates, 6 g fat (2.4 g sat fat), 1 g fiber

Lemon-Pepper Tilapia

Makes 4 servings • Prep time: 10 minutes • Total time: 18 minutes

1½ pounds tilapia

2 teaspoons olive oil

2 teaspoons lemon-pepper seasoning

1 teaspoon paprika (optional)

4 lemon slices

Lean proteins can help you feel more satisfied with fewer calories, which makes this tilapia dish a great choice for a quick weeknight meal. Its naturally mild flavor is anything but boring thanks to a little spice mix.

1. Cut a piece of parchment to fit the bottom of the air fryer basket and set aside. Preheat the air fryer to 400°F.

2. Brush the tilapia lightly with the oil and season both sides with the lemon-pepper seasoning and paprika (if using). Arrange the fish on the parchment so there is room between the pieces.

3. Air fry for 8 minutes until the fish is cooked through and flakes easily with a fork.

4. Serve with the lemon slices.

Per serving: 185 calories, 33 g protein, 0 g carbohydrates, 6 g fat (1.5 g sat fat), 0 g fiber

Fish Tacos with Quick-Pickled Onions and Peppers

Makes 4 servings • Prep time: 20 minutes • Total time: 35 minutes

QUICK-PICKLED ONIONS AND PEPPERS

1 small sweet onion, thinly sliced

1 small jalapeño pepper, seeded and sliced

⅓ cup apple cider vinegar

⅓ cup water

1 teaspoon salt

2 teaspoons sugar

FISH TACOS

1½ pounds cod

Salt and freshly ground black pepper

¼ cup all-purpose flour

2 large eggs

1 cup panko breadcrumbs

¼ cup light mayonnaise

1 tablespoon chipotle hot sauce

8 small flour tortillas

2 tablespoons chopped fresh cilantro

2 tablespoons chopped red onion (optional)

This dish has several components, but each is relatively quick to prepare and the results are truly worth it. If you have any leftover pickled onions, cover and refrigerate for up to a week and use in salads and sandwiches.

1. To make the quick-pickled onions and peppers: In a bowl, stir together the onion, jalapeño, vinegar, water, salt, and sugar. Let sit while you prepare the tacos.

2. Preheat the air fryer to 400°F.

3. To make the fish tacos: Season the cod with salt and pepper and sprinkle with flour, tossing until the fish is thoroughly coated; set aside.

4. In a shallow bowl, lightly beat the eggs. In a second shallow bowl, place the breadcrumbs. Working with a few pieces at a time, dip the fish into the egg mixture followed by the breadcrumbs. Press to ensure an even coating.

5. Working in batches if necessary, arrange the fish in a single layer in the air fryer basket and spritz lightly with olive oil. Air fry for 12 to 15 minutes, pausing halfway through the cooking time to turn the fish, until the fish flakes easily with a fork.

6. Meanwhile, in a small bowl, whisk together the mayonnaise and hot sauce. Slather the sauce on the tortillas and top with the fish, pickled onions, cilantro, and red onion (if using).

Per serving: 530 calories, 38 g protein, 60 g carbohydrates, 12 g fat (2.2 g sat fat), 2 g fiber

Stacked Black Bean Enchiladas

Makes 4 servings • Prep time: 15 minutes • Total time: 35 minutes

1 (15-ounce) can black beans, rinsed and drained

¼ red bell pepper, finely chopped

3 scallions, thinly sliced

1 tablespoon chili powder

1 (10-ounce) can enchilada sauce, red or green, divided

8 (6-inch) corn tortillas

½ cup reduced-free sour cream

½ cup reduced-fat shredded Cheddar

¼ cup chopped fresh cilantro

Depending on the size of your air fryer, fitting a rectangular dish full of enchiladas can be tricky. Instead, this recipe layers the ingredients into a round baking dish more like a lasagna. Problem solved! As an added bonus, you don't have to preheat the corn tortillas to avoid breaking them as you roll them up.

1. In a large bowl, stir together the beans, bell pepper, scallions, and chili powder until thoroughly combined.

2. Preheat the air fryer to 350°F.

3. Coat the inside of a 7-inch (7-cup) round baking dish with olive oil and spread a few spoonfuls of the enchilada sauce evenly in the bottom of the dish. Top with 2 tortillas and spread the following ingredients in even layers: a third of the sour cream, a third of the bean mixture, a quarter of the remaining sauce, and 1 tablespoon of the cheese. Top with 2 tortillas and repeat the layers with the remaining ingredients, ending with 2 tortillas topped with the remaining sauce and cheese.

4. Place the baking dish in the air fryer basket. Air fry for 20 minutes until the cheese is melted and the sauce is bubbling. Let rest for 5 minutes.

5. Top with the cilantro just before serving.

Per serving: *320 calories, 15 g protein, 46 g carbohydrates, 9 g fat (4.4 g sat fat), 11 g fiber*

Vegetarian Shepherd's Pie

Makes 4 servings • Prep time: 10 minutes • Total time: 40 minutes

2 teaspoons olive oil

1 small onion, chopped

1 small carrot, chopped

Salt and freshly ground black pepper

1 (10-ounce) package frozen plant-based meat crumbles

½ cup crushed tomatoes

½ teaspoon dried thyme

1 cup frozen peas

2 cups mashed potatoes

½ cup reduced-fat Cheddar cheese

Need an easy comfort casserole that comes together with a few items from your freezer and pantry? This vegetarian recipe is a surefire winner for the air fryer.

1. Combine the olive oil, onion, and carrot in a 7-inch (7-cup) round baking dish and stir until the vegetables are coated. Season to taste with salt and pepper.

2. Place the baking dish in the air fryer basket and set the air fryer to 350°F. Air fry for 5 minutes until the onion begins to soften.

3. Carefully add the meat crumbles and air fry for 5 minutes longer until the crumbles begin to sizzle. Add the tomatoes and thyme and stir until thoroughly combined. Scatter the peas on top of the vegetable mixture and spread the mashed potatoes on top.

4. Air fry for 15 minutes until heated throughout. Scatter the cheese on top and air fry for 5 minutes longer until melted.

Per serving: 330 calories, 25 g protein, 28 g carbohydrates, 10 g fat (3 g sat fat), 5 g fiber

Cauliflower "Steaks"
with Chimichurri Sauce

Makes 2 servings • Prep time: 10 minutes • Total time: 35 minutes

CAULIFLOWER "STEAKS"

1 large head cauliflower

2 teaspoons olive oil

Salt and freshly ground black pepper

CHIMICHURRI SAUCE

2 tablespoons olive oil

2 teaspoons red wine vinegar

2 tablespoons freshly chopped parsley

2 tablespoons freshly chopped cilantro

1 clove garlic, minced

½ teaspoon dried oregano

½ teaspoon red pepper flakes

Salt to taste

Cauliflower is notably low in calories and high in fiber (about 115 calories and 9 grams of fiber per pound)—the reason it plays a starring role in so many weight-loss recipes. However, it can be hard to get each piece perfectly browned, which is why this particular dish is so well suited to preparing in an air fryer.

1. Preheat the air fryer to at 450°F.

2. To make the cauliflower "steaks": Remove any outer leaves from the cauliflower and trim the stem of its cut edges, but leave the stem intact. Place on a cutting board stem-side down. Using a large chef's knife, cut two ½- to ¾-inch-thick slices from the center of the cauliflower (save the remaining cauliflower for another use). Rub the cauliflower with the olive oil and season to taste with salt and pepper.

3. Arrange the cauliflower in the air fryer basket and air fry for 25 to 35 minutes, turning once halfway through, until browned and the stems feel tender when pierced with a knife.

4. To make the chimichurri sauce: In a small bowl, stir together the olive oil, vinegar, parsley, cilantro, garlic, oregano, and red pepper flakes. Season to taste with salt.

5. Spoon the sauce over the cauliflower steaks just before serving.

Per serving: 215 calories, 4 g protein, 12 g carbohydrates, 18 g fat (2.5 g sat fat), 5 g fiber

Portobello Pizzas

Makes 4 servings • Prep time: 10 minutes • Total time: 20 minutes

1 cup crushed tomatoes

2 cloves garlic, minced

1 teaspoon sugar

½ teaspoon dried oregano

¼ teaspoon red pepper flakes (optional)

2 tablespoons olive oil

4 large portobello mushrooms, stems removed and gills scraped out

Salt and freshly ground pepper

6 ounces fresh mozzarella, sliced

1 cup frozen, thawed spinach, squeezed dry

½ cup grated Parmesan cheese

1 tablespoon chopped fresh parsley

Craving the taste of a mushroom pizza? Skip the carbs and calories in a traditional crust and enjoy this super-easy healthier version instead.

1. Preheat the air fryer to 400°F.

2. In a small bowl, stir together the tomatoes, garlic, sugar, oregano, and red pepper flakes (if using).

3. Rub the olive oil over the portobello mushrooms until thoroughly coated. Sprinkle both sides with salt and pepper. Place top-side down on a clean work surface. Divide the sauce among the mushrooms and top with the mozzarella, spinach, and Parmesan.

4. Working in batches if necessary, transfer the mushrooms to the air fryer basket. Air fry for 10 to 14 minutes until the mushrooms are tender and the cheese has begun to brown. Top with the fresh parsley just before serving.

Per serving: 265 calories, 17 g protein, 11 g carbohydrates, 11 g fat (7.4 g sat fat), 3 g fiber

easy entertaining

Bruschetta with Roasted Tomatoes 99

Crispy Brussels Sprouts with Honey-Mustard Dipping Sauce 100

Fried Artichoke Hearts with Aioli 101

Spicy Sicilian Chicken Drumsticks 102

Stuffed Chicken Breasts 105

Roast Turkey with Cranberry Sauce 106

Pistachio-Crusted Chicken with Pomegranate Glaze 108

Hawaiian Pork Chops with Pineapple 109

Roast Beef with Horseradish Cream 111

Steak Tips with Mushrooms 112

Swordfish Steaks with Cucumber Salsa 113

Crab Cakes with Roasted Corn-Pepper Relish 114

Bruschetta
with Roasted Tomatoes

Makes 8 servings • Prep time: 10 minutes • Total time: 20 minutes

1 large clove garlic

8 slices French bread (about 8 ounces)

1 cup grape tomatoes, halved

1 tablespoon olive oil

Salt and freshly ground black pepper

¼ cup prepared pesto

2 ounces goat cheese, crumbled

Zest of 1 lemon

If you dread the idea of giving up bread in order to lose weight, this recipe is for you. Your air fryer makes it easy to control the amount of added fat that is usually loaded onto bruschetta. *Buon appetito!*

1. Preheat the air fryer to 350°F.

2. Slice the garlic in half and rub gently on each piece of bread.

3. Arrange the bread in the air fryer basket and spritz lightly with olive oil. Working in batches if necessary, air fry for 5 minutes until lightly browned. Transfer the bread to a serving plate.

4. Meanwhile, mince the garlic. In a small baking pan, stir together the garlic, tomatoes, and olive oil. Season to taste with salt and pepper. Air fry the tomato mixture for 5 minutes until the tomatoes are soft and beginning to blister.

5. Spread the bread with the pesto. Top with the tomato mixture, cheese, and lemon zest before serving.

Per serving: 160 calories, 6 g protein, 17 g carbohydrates, 8 g fat (2.4 g sat fat), 1 g fiber

Crispy Brussels Sprouts with Honey-Mustard Dipping Sauce

Makes 4 servings • Prep time: 10 minutes • Total time: 25 minutes

BRUSSELS SPROUTS

1 pound fresh Brussels sprouts

1 tablespoon olive oil

1 teaspoon dried thyme

Salt and freshly ground black pepper

HONEY-MUSTARD SAUCE

3 tablespoons Dijon mustard

3 tablespoons honey

If you find yourself ordering Brussels sprouts every time you see them on a restaurant menu, you'll be delighted making them at home for friends and family. A quick shake in an air fryer basket beats having to turn each piece when baking in a standard oven. If you're concerned about carbs, try dipping them in mustard (without the honey) and you'll save 13 grams of carbs.

1. Preheat the air fryer to 380°F.

2. To make the Brussels sprouts: Trim the Brussels sprouts and halve any that are larger than 1 inch wide. Transfer to a large bowl, drizzle with the olive oil, sprinkle with the thyme, and season to taste with salt and pepper. Toss until thoroughly coated.

3. Add the Brussels sprouts to the air fryer basket and shake into a single layer. Air fry for 15 minutes, pausing to shake the basket halfway through the cooking time, until browned and beginning to crisp.

4. To make the honey-mustard sauce: In a small bowl, whisk together the Dijon and honey until smooth. Serve with the Brussels sprouts for dipping.

Per serving: 135 calories, 4 g protein, 24 g carbohydrates, 4 g fat (0.6 g sat fat), 5 g fiber

Fried Artichoke Hearts with Aioli

Makes 4 servings • Prep time: 10 minutes • Total time: 17 minutes

FRIED ARTICHOKE HEARTS

2 tablespoons panko breadcrumbs

2 tablespoons grated Parmesan cheese

½ teaspoon dried oregano

½ teaspoon garlic powder

1 (14-ounce) can quartered artichokes packed in water, drained

1 tablespoon olive oil

Salt and freshly ground black pepper

AIOLI

¼ cup reduced-fat mayonnaise

2 teaspoons fresh lemon juice

1 to 2 cloves garlic, minced

Here's a delicious way to start a casual dinner party with friends. Unlike traditional deep-frying, which can often render artichokes a soggy mess, your air fryer guarantees perfect results every time.

1. Preheat the air fryer to 400°F.

2. To make the artichokes: In a small bowl, stir together the breadcrumbs, Parmesan, oregano, and garlic powder until combined.

3. Pat the artichoke hearts dry with a paper towel to remove excess moisture and place in a large bowl. Drizzle with the olive oil and toss to coat. Sprinkle the breadcrumb mixture over the artichokes, season to taste with salt and pepper, and toss again.

4. Arrange the artichokes in the air fryer basket in a single layer. Air fry for 8 minutes, pausing halfway through the cooking time to shake the basket, until the artichokes begin to brown and the edges are crispy.

5. To make the aioli: In a small bowl, whisk together the mayonnaise, lemon juice, and garlic. Serve with the artichoke hearts for dipping.

Per serving: 140 calories, 3 g protein, 10 g carbohydrates, 10 g fat (1.7 g sat fat), 5 g fiber

Spicy Sicilian Chicken Drumsticks

Makes 4 servings • Prep time: 5 minutes • Total time: 30 minutes + marinating time

1 cup Italian salad dressing

1 tablespoon minced fresh rosemary, plus additional for garnish (optional)

1 teaspoon red pepper flakes

2 cloves garlic, minced

8 chicken drumsticks, skin-on

Slim down your drumsticks as well as your time in the kitchen! The secret: create a flavorful marinade with a dressing jump-start and a few fresh add-ins. Prep this dish in the morning and you'll be rewarded with a super-simple and satisfying dinner. If you're counting carbs, serve with a side salad and spiralized zucchini ribbons instead of traditional pasta.

1. In a large resealable bag, combine the salad dressing, rosemary, red pepper flakes, garlic, and chicken. Massage the bag to ensure the chicken is thoroughly coated; refrigerate for at least 2 hours or up to overnight.

2. Preheat the air fryer to 360°F.

3. Working in batches if necessary, arrange the drumsticks in the air fryer basket, making sure they do not touch. Discard the marinade. Air fry for 30 to 35 minutes, pausing halfway through the cooking time to turn the chicken, or until the skin is browned and a meat thermometer inserted into the thickest portion reaches 165°F.

4. Serve with additional rosemary sprigs as garnish (if using).

Per serving: 435 calories, 49 g protein, 0.5 g carbohydrates, 25 g fat (6.2 g sat fat), 0 g fiber

Stuffed Chicken Breasts

Makes 4 servings • Prep time: 20 minutes • Total time: 45 minutes

1 (5-ounce) bag fresh spinach

1 shallot, finely chopped

2 tablespoons olive oil, divided

2 tablespoons raisins, finely chopped

1 tablespoon chopped fresh rosemary

Salt and freshly ground black pepper

4 small boneless, skinless chicken breast halves (about 1½ pounds)

Juice of ½ lemon

Why dirty more pans than necessary? Your air fryer is the perfect tool for cooking fresh spinach for this flavorful dish. Less mess is the key to stress-free entertaining.

1. Preheat the air fryer to 360°F.

2. Place the spinach and shallot in a small pan and drizzle with 1 tablespoon of the olive oil. Place the pan in the air fryer basket and air fry for 5 minutes until the spinach is wilted, pausing halfway through the cooking time to stir the spinach. Transfer the spinach and shallot to a bowl and increase the air fryer temperature to 400°F.

3. Stir the raisins and rosemary into the spinach mixture and season to taste with salt and pepper.

4. Using a sharp knife, cut the chicken breasts, slicing them across and opening them up like a book, but be careful not to cut them all the way through. Sprinkle the chicken with salt and pepper.

5. Spoon equal amounts of the spinach mixture onto each chicken breast, then fold the chicken breast over the top of the stuffing. Secure the chicken with toothpicks and drizzle with the remaining 1 tablespoon of oil.

6. Working in batches if necessary, air fry the chicken for 18 to 20 minutes until cooked through and a meat thermometer inserted into the thickest part of the chicken reaches 165°F. Squeeze the lemon juice over the chicken breasts right after taking them out of the air fryer. Let rest for 5 minutes and remove the toothpicks before serving.

Per serving: 285 calories, 40 g protein, 7 g carbohydrates, 11 g fat (2.2 g sat fat), 1 g fiber

Roast Turkey with Cranberry Sauce

Makes 8 servings • Prep time: 10 minutes • Total time: 1 hour

ROAST TURKEY

1 teaspoon salt

1 teaspoon garlic powder

½ teaspoon dried rosemary

½ teaspoon paprika

½ teaspoon freshly ground black pepper

1 boneless, skinless turkey breast (about 3 pounds)

1 tablespoon olive oil

CRANBERRY SAUCE

1 (12-ounce) bag cranberries, fresh or frozen

½ cup frozen orange juice concentrate, thawed

2 tablespoons maple syrup

¼ cup water (if needed)

An air fryer can give you so much more flexibility during the holidays, freeing up valuable space in your regular oven for other dishes. But why wait for the holidays when such a delicious meal can fit into your weight loss plans any time of year?

1. To make the roast turkey: In a small bowl, stir together the salt, garlic powder, rosemary, paprika, and pepper.

2. Coat the turkey breast with the olive oil on all sides and rub with the seasoning mixture until thoroughly coated. Place the turkey breast in the air fryer basket and air fry at 350°F for 40 minutes, pausing halfway through to flip the turkey breast, until a meat thermometer inserted into the thickest portion reaches 165°F.

3. To make the cranberry sauce: In a small pot, combine the cranberries, orange juice concentrate, and maple syrup over medium-high heat until the mixture begins to boil. Reduce the heat and simmer, stirring occasionally, for 20 minutes, until most of the cranberries have burst. Add water, 1 tablespoon at a time, if you prefer a thinner sauce.

4. Transfer the turkey to a cutting board and allow to rest 15 minutes before slicing and serving with the sauce.

TIP: Given the longer roasting time, there's no need to preheat your air fryer with this dish.

Per serving: 260 calories, 39 g protein, 14 g carbohydrates, 4 g fat (1 g sat fat), 2 g fiber

Pistachio-Crusted Chicken with Pomegranate Glaze

Makes 4 servings • Prep time: 10 minutes • Total time: 20 minutes

2 boneless, skinless chicken breasts (about 1½ pounds)

Salt and freshly ground black pepper

¼ cup reduced-fat mayonnaise

½ cup chopped shelled pistachios

1 (5-ounce) bag baby arugula

2 tablespoons pomegranate or balsamic glaze, for garnish

Some research suggests that eating nuts regularly may play an important role in helping you lose weight because they are loaded with monounsaturated fats. However, the real reason to enjoy them is because they are so delicious! Instead of using eggs and flour to make an air fryer feast, this dish relies on reduced-calorie mayonnaise to help the nuts form a crunchy coating.

1. Cut a piece of parchment paper to fit the bottom of the air fryer basket. Preheat the air fryer to 400°F.

2. Starting on the thicker side, use a long, sharp knife to slice each chicken breast horizontally, cutting until you›ve reached the other side, to make 4 cutlets. Season with salt and pepper. Spread a thin layer of mayonnaise on both sides of the cutlets.

3. Place the pistachios in a shallow dish and dredge the chicken in the nuts, pressing gently to form an even coating. Arrange the cutlets on the parchment paper in the air fryer basket so they're not touching. Air fry for 8 to 10 minutes until browned and cooked through.

4. Let rest for 5 minutes before serving on a bed of arugula, drizzled with the glaze for garnish.

Per serving: 360 calories, 43 g protein, 8 g carbohydrates, 18 g fat (3 g sat fat), 2 g fiber

Hawaiian Pork Chops with Pineapple

Makes 4 servings • Prep time: 10 minutes • Total time: 20 minutes + marinating time

3 tablespoons
Worcestershire sauce

1 tablespoon
brown sugar

1 tablespoon grated
fresh ginger

½ teaspoon red pepper
flakes (optional)

4 center-cut boneless
pork chops (about
1½ pounds)

4 slices fresh pineapple,
each about ½ inch thick

2 scallions, thinly sliced

Pork and pineapple are the perfect combination, especially when you use an air fryer—the pineapple will caramelize as it cooks on top of the meat. Serve on a bed of brown rice or alongside a colorful coleslaw salad.

1. In a shallow dish, stir together the Worcestershire sauce, brown sugar, ginger, and red pepper flakes (if using) until smooth. Add the pork, turning to coat, and marinate at room temperature for 30 minutes, turning once.

2. Preheat the air fryer to 400°F.

3. Arrange the pork in the air fryer basket so the pieces do not touch and spritz lightly with olive oil. Air fry for 10 minutes, pausing halfway through the cooking time to turn the chops and set a pineapple ring on top of each chop, until browned and a meat thermometer inserted into the thickest portion reaches 145°F.

4. Let rest for 5 minutes before serving topped with the scallions.

Per serving: 325 calories, 38 g protein, 13 g carbohydrates, 13 g fat (4.6 g sat fat), 1 g fiber

Roast Beef
with Horseradish Cream

Makes 6 servings • Prep time: 10 minutes • Total time: 45 minutes

ROAST BEEF

2 pounds beef roast top round or eye of round

1 tablespoon salt

2 teaspoons garlic powder

1 teaspoon freshly ground black pepper

1 teaspoon dried thyme

HORSERADISH CREAM

⅓ cup fat-free half-and-half

⅓ cup reduced-fat sour cream

⅓ cup prepared horseradish

2 teaspoons fresh lemon juice

Salt and freshly ground black pepper

A classic beef roast is an easy way to impress guests without derailing your weight loss goals. Serve with a simple salad or the Crispy Brussels Sprouts on page 100.

1. Preheat the air fryer to 400°F.

2. To make the roast beef: Season the beef with the salt, garlic powder, pepper, and thyme. Place the beef fat-side down in the air fryer basket and lightly spritz with olive oil. Air fry for 35 to 45 minutes, pausing halfway through the cooking time to turn the beef, until a meat thermometer inserted into the thickest part indicates the desired doneness, 125°F (rare) to 150°F (medium). Let the beef rest for 10 minutes before slicing.

3. To make the horseradish cream: In a small bowl, whisk together the half-and-half, sour cream, horseradish, and lemon juice until thoroughly combined. Season to taste with salt and pepper. Serve alongside the beef.

Per serving: 235 calories, 35 g protein, 4 g carbohydrates, 8 g fat (3.3 g sat fat), 0 g fiber

Steak Tips with Mushrooms

Makes 4 servings • Prep time: 10 minutes • Total time: 20 minutes + marinating time

1½ pounds sirloin, trimmed and cut into 1-inch pieces

8 ounces brown mushrooms, halved

¼ cup Worcestershire sauce

1 tablespoon Dijon mustard

1 tablespoon olive oil

1 teaspoon paprika

1 teaspoon red pepper flakes

¼ red onion, thinly sliced

2 tablespoons chopped fresh parsley (optional)

Cooking steak in an air fryer can be tricky because it's easy to accidentally overcook the meat. This recipe gives you a little more wiggle room because the marinade helps keep the steak tender and juicy. For a true steakhouse experience, serve with baked potatoes and a wedge salad.

1. Place the beef and mushrooms in a large resealable bag. In a small bowl, whisk together the Worcestershire, mustard, olive oil, paprika, and red pepper flakes. Add the onion and stir to combine. Pour the marinade into the bag and massage gently to ensure the beef and mushrooms are evenly coated. Seal the bag and refrigerate for at least 4 hours, preferably overnight. Remove from the refrigerator 30 minutes before cooking.

2. Preheat the air fryer to 400°F.

3. Drain and discard the marinade. Arrange the steak and mushrooms in the air fryer basket. Air fry for 10 minutes, pausing halfway through the baking time to shake the basket, until the mushrooms are browned and the steak tips are cooked to the desired doneness when tested with a meat thermometer, 125°F (rare) to 150°F (medium). Transfer to a serving plate and top with the parsley (if using).

Per serving: 330 calories, 41 g protein, 2 g carbohydrates, 17 g fat (6.2 g sat fat), 0 g fiber

Swordfish Steaks with Cucumber Salsa

Makes 2 servings • Prep time: 20 minutes • Total time: 30 minutes

SWORDFISH

2 teaspoons honey

2 teaspoons reduced-sodium soy sauce

2 swordfish steaks (about 12 ounces)

CUCUMBER SALSA

1 cucumber, peeled, seeded, and chopped

½ jalapeño pepper, seeded and finely chopped

1 scallion, thinly sliced

Juice of ½ lime

2 tablespoons chopped fresh mint or cilantro

Salt and freshly ground black pepper

This easy honey-soy marinade works well with most fish, but the cucumber salsa is a perfect complement to the rich, oily texture of swordfish. You can use either mint or cilantro in the salsa, whichever you prefer.

1. To make the swordfish: In a shallow dish, stir together the honey and soy sauce until smooth. Add the swordfish, turning to coat, and marinate at room temperature for 15 minutes, turning once. Preheat the air fryer to 400°F while the fish marinates.

2. To make the cucumber salsa: In a small bowl, stir together the cucumber, jalapeño, scallion, lime juice, and mint or cilantro. Season to taste with salt and pepper.

3. Place the fish in the air fryer basket and spritz with olive oil. Air fry for 10 minutes, pausing halfway through the cooking time to flip the fish, until cooked through and a fork slips easily through the fish.

4. Serve the swordfish topped with the salsa.

TIP: To minimize mercury exposure, most health experts recommend limiting your intake of large fish like swordfish (pregnant women should avoid it altogether), but for special occasions swordfish is a fitting treat.

Per serving: 265 calories, 31 g protein, 10 g carbohydrates, 10 g fat (2.5 g sat fat), 1 g fiber

Crab Cakes with Roasted Corn-Pepper Relish

Makes 4 servings • Prep time: 20 minutes • Total time: 35 minutes

ROASTED CORN-PEPPER RELISH

1 (8.75-ounce) can sweet corn, drained

¼ red bell pepper, seeded and finely chopped

1 teaspoon sugar

1 tablespoon rice wine vinegar

1 teaspoon unsalted butter

CRAB CAKES

8 ounces lump crabmeat

2 large eggs, beaten

1 cup panko breadcrumbs, divided

5 tablespoons reduced-fat mayonnaise, divided

1 tablespoon Dijon mustard

1 teaspoon Old Bay seasoning

½ teaspoon salt

1 tablespoon chipotle hot sauce

Zest of 1 lemon

Chopped fresh parsley, for garnish

These crab cakes are sure to draw rave reviews whether you serve them as a main dish or an appetizer. For appetizer-size portions, shape the crab mixture into smaller patties and reduce the time in the air fryer to 5 to 7 minutes.

1. Preheat the air fryer to 350°F.

2. To make the relish: In a small baking pan, combine the corn, bell pepper, and sugar. Air fry for 5 minutes until the pepper is softened. Remove from the air fryer and stir in the vinegar and butter. Set aside and continue to preheat the air fryer.

3. Meanwhile, to make the crab cakes: In a large bowl, combine the crabmeat, eggs, ½ cup of the breadcrumbs, 3 tablespoons of the mayonnaise, Dijon, Old Bay seasoning, and salt.

4. Use an ice cream scoop to form the crab mixture patties. Place the patties on a piece of parchment paper cut to fit the dimensions of your air fryer basket, then press lightly with the bottom of the scoop to flatten the patties into a circle about ½ inch thick. Press the remaining ½ cup of breadcrumbs on top and spritz lightly with olive oil. Air fry for 10 minutes until lightly browned.

5. In a small bowl, combine the remaining 2 tablespoons of mayonnaise and the chipotle sauce, stirring until smooth.

6. Serve the crab cakes over the corn-pepper relish and top with the chipotle sauce, lemon zest, and parsley.

Per serving: 335 calories, 19 g protein, 34 g carbohydrates, 12 g fat (2.6 g sat fat), 1 g fiber

sweet treats

Glazed Doughnuts **119**

Cinnamon Apple Chips **120**

Caramel-Pecan Popcorn **121**

Almond Cookies **122**

Peanut Butter Chocolate Chip Cookies **125**

Chocolate Lava Cake for Two **126**

Cheesecake Bites **127**

Strawberry Shortcake **128**

Cherry Hand Pies **131**

Baked Apples **132**

Honey-Roasted Bananas **133**

Almond-Stuffed Peaches **134**

Blueberry Crisp **137**

Glazed Doughnuts

Makes 4 doughnuts • Prep time: 10 minutes • Total time: 17 minutes

DOUGHNUTS

1 cup all-purpose flour

1½ teaspoons baking powder

½ teaspoon salt

¾ cup vanilla nonfat Greek yogurt

GLAZE

½ cup powdered sugar

1 tablespoon unsalted butter, melted

½ teaspoon vanilla extract

1½ teaspoons hot water

1 or 2 drops food coloring (optional)

Edible cake decorations (optional)

Decadent doughnuts don't need to take all day or consume all your daily calories! Traditional yeast doughnuts work well in an air fryer, but they require extra time to let the dough rise. A ready-to-go package of biscuit dough makes for speedier prep, but this easy recipe offers an even better way to make your doughnuts lower in fat and just as delicious.

1. To make the doughnuts: In a large bowl, stir together the flour, baking powder, and salt. Add the yogurt and mix until shaggy, then knead in the bowl until the dough holds together in a ball.

2. Divide the dough into 4 equal pieces. On a lightly floured work surface, roll each piece into a ball and pat into a disk about ½ inch thick. Poke your finger through the center of each disk to form into a doughnut shape.

3. Place the doughnuts in the air fryer with space between them. Spray the doughnuts lightly with cooking spray. Air fry for 7 minutes at 350°F, flipping halfway through, until golden brown.

4. To make the glaze: In a small bowl, stir together the powdered sugar, butter, vanilla, and water until smooth. Stir in the food coloring (if using).

5. When the doughnuts are cool enough to handle, dip the tops into the glaze and sprinkle on decorations (if using). Serve warm.

Per serving: 240 calories, 8 g protein, 44 g carbohydrates, 3.5 g fat (2 g sat fat), 1 g fiber

Cinnamon Apple Chips

Makes 4 servings • Prep time: 5 minutes • Cook time: 20–25 minutes

2 tablespoons unsalted butter, melted

1 tablespoon brown sugar

½ teaspoon ground cinnamon

Pinch of salt

2 large apples, such as Gala, Fuji, or Honeycrisp, cored

Delicious and true: chips can be part of your skinny lifestyle! Your air fryer makes a crunchy and sweet treat out of classic apples. It's an easy way to mix up your snack routine while reaching your fruit and vegetable goals.

1. In a large bowl, stir together the butter, brown sugar, cinnamon, and salt.

2. Slice the apples into thin disks using a mandoline slicer, or slice as thinly as possible using a knife.

3. Gently toss the apple slices with the butter mixture until thoroughly coated.

4. Place the apple slices in the air fryer basket, making sure they don't overlap. Set to 360°F and air fry in batches until crispy, about 20 to 25 minutes, pausing once or twice during the cooking time to shake the basket and flip the chips.

5. The chips will become crispier as they cool. Store in a covered container at room temperature.

Per serving: 140 calories, 0 g protein, 21 g carbohydrates, 6 g fat (4 g sat fat), 2.5 g fiber

Caramel-Pecan Popcorn

Makes 4 servings • Prep time: 10 minutes • Total time: 1 hour

3 cups air-popped popcorn

¼ cup chopped pecans

¼ cup packed dark brown sugar

2 tablespoons light-colored corn syrup

1 tablespoon unsalted butter

¼ teaspoon vanilla extract

⅛ teaspoon baking soda

⅛ teaspoon salt

It's easy to get swept away by the high heat of an air fryer. But you can produce magical results at a lower temperature, too. Caramel popcorn is a gourmet treat at a fraction of the store-bought cost (and calories).

1. Place the popcorn and nuts in a large bowl and set aside. Generously spritz the air fryer basket with a neutral-flavored oil, such as avocado. Line a baking sheet with parchment paper.

2. In a small, heavy-bottomed saucepan over medium heat, combine the brown sugar, corn syrup, and butter and bring to a boil. Cook 2 to 3 minutes, stirring three or four times to scrape down the sides of the pan and keep the mixture from bubbling up. If you have a pastry brush, dip it in cool water and use it to brush down the sides of the pan. Remove from the heat; stir in the vanilla, baking soda, and salt.

3. Preheat the air fryer to 250°F.

4. Carefully pour the sugar mixture over the popcorn in a steady stream, stirring with a silicone spatula until thoroughly coated.

5. Transfer the popcorn mixture to the air fryer basket. Air fry for 45 minutes, stirring every 15 minutes with a silicone spatula, until the mixture begins to look dry.

6. Spread the popcorn on the prepared baking sheet, breaking up any large clumps. The popcorn will harden as it cools. Store in an airtight container for up to 1 week.

Per serving: 180 calories, 1 g protein, 28 g carbohydrates, 8 g fat (2.3 g sat fat), 2 g fiber

Almond Cookies

Makes 18 cookies • Prep time: 10 minutes • Total time: 35 minutes

2 cups almonds

1 cup sugar

2 large egg whites

½ teaspoon almond extract

Bite into the crunchy exterior of these delicious cookies and you'll find a sweet chewy interior. Use blanched (skinless) almonds if you prefer lighter colored cookies, but if you're in a pinch regular almonds will taste just as wonderful.

1. Cut a piece of parchment to fit the air fryer basket, and preheat the air fryer to 300°F.

2. In a food processor, grind the almonds into a fine meal. Add the sugar and whirl for another 15 seconds. Add the egg whites and almond extract and continue to whirl for another 15 seconds until a smooth dough forms around the blade.

3. Using a teaspoon, shape the dough into 18 equal portions. Working in batches, arrange the cookies in the air fryer so they are at least 1½ inches apart. Air fry for 25 to 30 minutes, pausing halfway through the baking time to flatten the cookies slightly with the back of a spoon, until golden.

TIP: Just four ingredients create amazing, gluten-free cookies!

Per cookie: 135 calories, 4 g protein, 15 g carbohydrates, 8 g fat (0.6 g sat fat), 2 g fiber

Peanut Butter Chocolate Chip Cookies

Makes 16 cookies • Prep time: 5 minutes • Total time: 10 minutes

1 cup creamy peanut butter

1 cup packed brown sugar

1 large egg

½ teaspoon vanilla extract

½ cup semisweet mini chocolate chips

Five-ingredient cookies that taste amazingly rich? You bet! Your air fryer makes it easy to whip up small batches of homemade treats, giving you the power to satisfy your cravings—without having dozens of extra cookies lingering around the kitchen to tempt you further. If you're serious about watching carbs, this recipe works well with sugar replacements, such as Swerve.

1. Preheat the air fryer to 350°F. Lightly spritz the air fryer basket with a neutral-flavored oil, such as avocado.

2. In a large bowl, combine the peanut butter, brown sugar, egg, and vanilla. Using a mixer, beat until thoroughly combined. Stir in the chocolate chips and divide the dough into 16 equal pieces.

3. Shape the dough into balls and flatten slightly with the back of a spoon.

4. Working in batches if necessary, arrange the cookies in the air fryer basket so they are not touching. Air fry for 5 minutes until browned. Let cool in the basket for 5 minutes before carefully transferring to a rack to finish cooling.

Per cookie: 180 calories, 4 g protein, 21 g carbohydrates, 10 g fat (2.7 g sat fat), 1 g fiber

Chocolate Lava Cake for Two

Makes 2 servings • Prep time: 10 minutes • Total time: 20 minutes

¼ cup semisweet chocolate chips (about 1½ ounces)

2 tablespoons unsalted butter

¼ cup powdered sugar

1 large egg

¼ teaspoon vanilla extract

Pinch of salt

1 tablespoon all-purpose flour

½ cup fresh raspberries

Need a dessert for a romantic night? This fancy lava cake is designed to share from the same plate. The key to success is not overbaking the cake so that the rich chocolate center oozes out when you cut into it with your fork. It's definitely one to save for special occasions, but the splurge is worth it.

1. Preheat the air fryer to 370°F. Lightly spritz an 8-ounce ramekin with a neutral-flavored oil, such as avocado.

2. In a large microwave-safe bowl, combine the chocolate chips and butter. Microwave on high for 1 minute until the butter is melted and the chips are beginning to melt. Whisk until smooth.

3. Add the powdered sugar, egg, vanilla, and salt and whisk until smooth. Add the flour and stir just until the flour is incorporated. Transfer the chocolate mixture to the prepared ramekin.

4. Place the ramekin in the air fryer basket. Air fry for 8 to 10 minutes until the top appears slightly puffed and dry. Let rest for about 1 minute.

5. Use a butter knife to loosen the sides and turn over onto a plate. Serve garnished with the raspberries.

Per serving: 335 calories, 5 g protein, 36 g carbohydrates, 21 g fat (12 g sat fat), 3 g fiber

Cheesecake Bites

Makes 15 servings • Prep time: 10 minutes • Total time: 20 minutes + chilling time

1 (1.9-ounce) package mini phyllo pastry shells

1 (4-ounce) package Neufchâtel

¼ cup sugar

1 tablespoon fresh lemon zest

½ cup fat-free nondairy whipped topping

15 fresh raspberries

Headed to a party? Make a batch of these dainty cheesecake bites to take along and you're guaranteed to have something delicious for you to enjoy without blowing your calorie budget.

1. Preheat the air fryer to 350°F.

2. Working in batches if necessary, arrange the pastry shells in the air fryer basket and spritz lightly with a neutral-flavored oil, such as avocado oil. Air fry for 5 to 7 minutes until golden. Transfer to a baking sheet and let cool completely before filling.

3. Meanwhile, using a mixer fitted with a paddle attachment, beat the Neufchâtel, sugar, and lemon zest until smooth. Use a silicone spatula to carefully fold the whipped topping into the cheese mixture until thoroughly combined.

4. Fill each shell with about a scant tablespoon of the cheese mixture and top with a raspberry. Cover and refrigerate for 2 hours before serving.

TIP: Look for mini phyllo pastry shells in your grocery's freezer case.

Per serving: 50 calories, 1 g protein, 7 g carbohydrates, 2 g fat (1 g sat fat), 0 g fiber

Strawberry Shortcake

Makes 4 servings • Prep time: 20 minutes • Total time: 32 minutes

2 cups sliced strawberries (about 1 pint)

1 tablespoon honey

¾ cup all-purpose flour, plus more for dusting

2 tablespoons sugar

¾ teaspoon baking powder

¼ teaspoon salt

2 tablespoons unsalted butter

⅓ cup low-fat buttermilk

1 large egg, lightly beaten

½ teaspoon vanilla extract

1 cup fat-free nondairy whipped topping

Nothing says summer like strawberry shortcake! It's the perfect way to end a cookout, and your air fryer is guaranteed to make it so very easy. Letting the strawberries sit in the honey for a bit will draw out the sweetest juices.

1. In a large bowl, combine the strawberries and honey. Stir until the strawberries are thoroughly coated. Set aside.

2. Preheat the air fryer to 400°F.

3. In another large bowl, stir together the flour, sugar, baking powder, and salt. Add the butter and work it into the flour mixture with your fingers until it resembles coarse meal.

4. In a small bowl, whisk together the buttermilk, egg, and vanilla. Add to the flour mixture and stir until a dough forms.

5. Turn the dough out onto a lightly floured work surface and divide into 4 pieces. Shape each piece into a biscuit about ½ inch thick.

6. Arrange the biscuits in the air fryer basket so they are not touching. Air fry for 12 to 15 minutes until golden. When the biscuits are cool enough to handle, split in half.

7. Divide the strawberries and any accumulated juices among the biscuits and top with whipped topping before serving.

Per serving: 290 calories, 7 g protein, 48 g carbohydrates, 9 g fat (4.9 g sat fat), 4 g fiber

Cherry Hand Pies

Makes 8 servings • Prep time: 20 minutes • Total time: 30 minutes

1 (14-ounce) package refrigerated pie crust

½ cup all-fruit cherry preserves

1 large egg, lightly beaten

2 tablespoons sugar

Traditional pies are tricky to bake in an air fryer because, unlike a conventional oven, the heating element is positioned in the top of the unit so the bottom crust has little opportunity to become crisp. These tender, flaky hand pies, however, cook quickly and benefit from the hot air that circulates all around them.

1. Preheat the air fryer to 350°F.

2. Roll out the pie crusts on a lightly floured surface. Trim each crust into a square and cut into 4 smaller squares for a total of 8 squares (discard the edges).

3. Place a tablespoon of preserves in the center of each square. Working one at a time, fold one corner of the dough over and press against the opposite corner to form a triangle. Use a fork to crimp the edges. Use the tip of a knife to cut a small hole in the top so steam can escape. Brush the pies with the egg and sprinkle with the sugar.

4. In batches if necessary, arrange the pies in the air fryer basket so they are not touching. Air fry for 8 to 10 minutes until golden. Serve warm or at room temperature.

Per serving: 300 calories, 3 g protein, 30 g carbohydrates, 15 g fat (5.7 g sat fat), 1 g fiber

Baked Apples

2 Honeycrisp apples

¼ cup chopped pecans

2 tablespoons brown sugar

1 tablespoon unsalted butter, softened

1 tablespoon golden raisins

Pinch of ground cinnamon

Pinch of salt

Most air fryer baskets have a drip pan beneath them. Adding a little water to the basket helps create steam that will transform these apples into a delicious dessert without becoming soggy. If you're more of a pear fan, this recipe works just as well with pears, too.

1. Preheat the air fryer to 350°F.

2. Cut the apples in half and use a melon baller to remove the core and some of the flesh (leave the skin on).

3. In a small bowl, stir together the pecans, brown sugar, butter, raisins, cinnamon, and salt. Fill the apple cavities with the nut mixture, pressing gently to ensure the filling holds its shape.

4. Pour ½ cup of water into the bottom of the air fryer basket to fill the drip pan. Arrange the apples in the air fryer basket. Air fry for 15 minutes until the apples are soft and the tops are beginning to brown.

Per serving: 165 calories, 1 g protein, 24 g carbohydrates, 8 g fat (2.2 g sat fat), 4 g fiber

Honey-Roasted Bananas

Makes 2 servings • Prep time: 5 minutes • Total time: 10 minutes

2 large bananas, peeled

1 tablespoon honey

Pinch of ground cinnamon

Craving something sweet? Your air fryer is the perfect appliance for transforming that plain-looking bunch of bananas on your counter into an amazing dessert. Serve with a small scoop of sugar-free vanilla ice cream for an extra treat.

1. Preheat the air fryer to 380°F. Cut a piece of parchment to fit the air fryer basket.

2. Slice the bananas in half lengthwise and arrange cut-side down on the parchment, leaving space in between so they are not touching. Drizzle with the honey and sprinkle with a pinch of cinnamon. Use your finger to spread the honey if necessary.

3. Air fry for 5 minutes until the bananas are beginning to brown.

Per serving: 155 calories, 2 g protein, 40 g carbohydrates, 0 g fat (0 g sat fat), 4 g fiber

Almond-Stuffed Peaches

Makes 4 servings • Prep time: 15 minutes • Total time: 45 minutes

2 large peaches

½ cup finely chopped almonds

1 large egg white

¼ cup packed brown sugar

¼ teaspoon almond extract

Pinch of ground cinnamon

Peaches are a tricky fruit because they continue to ripen after being picked. To enjoy peaches at the peak of ripeness, take a sniff. They should have a rich, strong scent. Other signs to look for are a deeper, golden yellow just around the stem and a slight yield when pressed gently with your thumb.

1. Preheat the air fryer to 350°F.

2. Cut the peaches in half and remove the pits (do not peel). Arrange cut-side up in a shallow baking dish that fits your air fryer.

3. In a small bowl, stir together the almonds, egg white, brown sugar, almond extract, and cinnamon until thoroughly combined.

4. Fill the cavities of each peach half with the almond mixture, pressing gently to ensure it holds its shape. Spritz lightly with a neutral-flavored cooking oil, such as avocado oil. Cover with foil.

5. Air fry for 25 minutes until the peaches are tender. Remove the foil and continue air frying for another 5 minutes until the tops are browned.

Per serving: *205 calories, 6 g protein, 28 g carbohydrates, 9 g fat (0.7 g sat fat), 4 g fiber*

Blueberry Crisp

Makes 6 servings • Prep time: 10 minutes • Total time: 50 minutes

1 cup rolled oats

¼ cup all-purpose flour

¼ cup packed
brown sugar

¼ teaspoon salt

3 tablespoons unsalted
butter, melted

4 cups fresh blueberries

¼ cup granulated sugar

1 tablespoon cornstarch

1 tablespoon fresh
lemon juice

¼ teaspoon
ground nutmeg

6 small scoops
no-sugar vanilla
ice cream (optional)

When summer blueberry season hits, this is the dessert you'll want to put at the top of your rotation. It's so easy to assemble, and with the convenience of an air fryer you'll hardly notice that you've got something baking until the aroma hits you.

1. Preheat the air fryer to 350°F. Lightly coat a 7-cup baking dish that fits in your air fryer with cooking spray. Set aside.

2. In a large bowl, stir together the oats, flour, brown sugar, and salt until thoroughly combined. Stir in the butter and mix with a fork until clumps begin to form. Set aside.

3. Place the blueberries in the prepared baking dish. Sprinkle with the granulated sugar, cornstarch, lemon juice, and nutmeg. Stir gently until the blueberries are coated. Spread into an even layer and top with the oat mixture.

4. Air fry for 40 minutes until the top is golden and the berries are bubbling. Let cool slightly before serving topped with ice cream (if using).

Per serving: *250 calories, 3 g protein, 46 g carbohydrates, 7 g fat (3.8 g sat fat), 4 g fiber*

index

A

Aioli, 101
air fryer benefits, 4–5
almonds
    Almond Cookies, 122
    Almond-Stuffed Peaches, 134
appetizers
    Bruschetta with Roasted Tomatoes, 99
    Crab Rangoon, 39
    Crispy Brussels Sprouts with Honey-Mustard Dipping Sauce, 100
    Fried Cauliflower with Spicy Dipping Sauce, 29
    Guilt-Free Veggie Egg Rolls, 38
    Healthier Mozzarella Sticks, 31
    Herbed Ricotta Bites, 30
apples
    Apple Dutch Baby Pancake, 15
    Baked Apples, 132
    Cinnamon Apple Chips, 120
Apricot Glaze, Pork Tenderloin with, 68
Artichoke Hearts with Aioli, Fried, 101
Asian-inspired foods
    Asian Pork Salad, 58
    Chinese Chicken Patties, 55
    General Tso's Chicken, 54
    Korean Beef in Lettuce Cups, 74
    Miso-Glazed Cod, 84
    Tandoori Chicken with Cucumber Raita, 50
    Thai Chicken Skewers with Peanut Sauce, 49
asparagus
    Bacon-Wrapped Asparagus, 41
    roasted, 70

avocado
    avocado oil, 6
    Chicken Cobb Salad with Buffalo Drizzle, 57
    Sunny-Side-Up Eggs in Avocado, 19

B

bacon
    Bacon-Wrapped Asparagus, 41
    Cheesy Bacon & Egg Cups, 16
Bananas, Honey-Roasted, 133
Barbecue-Glazed Salmon, 83
basil, 30
beans. See black beans; Chickpeas, Smoky
beef
    Homestyle Meatloaf, 76
    Korean Beef in Lettuce Cups, 74
    Roast Beef with Horseradish Cream, 111
    Steak Tips with Mushrooms, 112
    Stuffed Peppers, 75
berries
    Berry Creamy Breakfast Sandwiches, 21
    Blueberry Crisp, 137
    Cranberry Sauce, 106
    French Toast Cups with Raspberries, 14
    Strawberry Shortcake, 128
Biscuit Balls, Cheesy Sausage, 25
black beans
    as side dish, 22, 69
    Stacked Black Bean Enchiladas, 90
Blueberry Crisp, 137

bread
    Berry Creamy Breakfast Sandwiches, 21
    Bruschetta with Roasted Tomatoes, 99
    Cheesy Sausage Biscuit Balls, 25
    English Muffin Breakfast Pizzas, 20
    French Toast Cups with Raspberries, 14
breakfast bars, 13
breakfast sandwiches, 20, 21
Broccoli, Better-Than-Takeout Shrimp and, 82
Bruschetta with Roasted Tomatoes, 99
Brussels Sprouts with Honey-Mustard Dipping Sauce, Crispy, 100
Burgers, California-Style Turkey, 46

C

cabbage
    Cabbage Patties with Zucchini, 32
    Guilt-Free Veggie Egg Rolls, 38
cakes
    Cheesecake Bites, 127
    Chocolate Lava Cake for Two, 126
    Strawberry Shortcake, 128
California-Style Turkey Burgers, 46
calorie intake, 5–6
Calzones, Ham and Cheese, 73
Caramel-Pecan Popcorn, 121
carbohydrates, 7
Caribbean Chicken with Mango Salsa, 51
carrots
    Asian Pork Salad, 58
    California-Style Turkey Burgers, 46
cauliflower
    Cauliflower "Steaks" with Chimichurri Sauce, 93
    Fried Cauliflower with Spicy Dipping Sauce, 29
cheese
    Berry Creamy Breakfast Sandwiches, 21

Cheesecake Bites, 127
Cheesy Bacon & Egg Cups, 16
Cheesy Sausage Biscuit Balls, 25
Chicken Cobb Salad with Buffalo Drizzle, 57
Ham and Cheese Calzones, 73
Healthier Mozzarella Sticks, 31
Herbed Ricotta Bites, 30
Neufchâtel fat content, 39
cherries
    Cherry Hand Pies, 131
    Cherry-Oatmeal Bars, 13
chicken
    Breaded Chicken Tenders with Maple-Mustard Dipping Sauce, 78
    Caribbean Chicken with Mango Salsa, 51
    Chicken Cobb Salad with Buffalo Drizzle, 57
    Chicken Fajitas, 52
    Chicken Parmigiana, 62
    Chinese Chicken Patties, 55
    Favorite Lemon Chicken, 63
    General Tso's Chicken, 54
    Greek Meatballs with Tzatziki Sauce, 67
    Pistachio-Crusted Chicken with Pomegranate Glaze, 108
    Spicy Sicilian Chicken Drumsticks, 102
    Stuffed Chicken Breasts, 105
    Tandoori Chicken with Cucumber Raita, 50
    Thai Chicken Skewers with Peanut Sauce, 49
Chickpeas, Smoky, 42
Chilaquiles, Skinny, 22
Chimichurri Sauce, 93
Chinese-inspired foods. See Asian-inspired foods
chocolate
    Chocolate Lava Cake for Two, 126
    Peanut Butter Chocolate Chip Cookies, 125
Cinnamon Apple Chips, 120

Cod, Miso-Glazed, 84
cookies and bars
    Almond Cookies, 122
    Cherry-Oatmeal Bars, 13
    Peanut Butter Chocolate Chip
        Cookies, 125
Corn-Pepper Relish, Roasted, 114
crab
    Crab Cakes with Roasted Corn-Pepper
        Relish, 114
    Crab Rangoon, 39
Cranberry Sauce, 106
Cuban Tenderloin, 69
cucumber
    Asian Pork Salad, 58
    Cucumber Raita, 50
    Cucumber Salsa, 113
    Tzatziki Sauce, 67

D

desserts and treats. *See also* snacks
    Almond Cookies, 122
    Almond-Stuffed Peaches, 134
    Baked Apples, 132
    Blueberry Crisp, 137
    Cheesecake Bites, 127
    Cherry Hand Pies, 131
    Chocolate Lava Cake for Two, 126
    Glazed Doughnuts, 119
    Honey-Roasted Bananas, 133
    Peanut Butter Chocolate Chip
        Cookies, 125
    Strawberry Shortcake, 128
Doughnuts, Glazed, 119

E

Egg Rolls, Guilt-Free Veggie, 38
eggs
    Cheesy Bacon & Egg Cups, 16
    Chicken Cobb Salad with Buffalo
        Drizzle, 57
    Skinny Chilaquiles, 22
    Sunny-Side-Up Eggs in Avocado, 19
Enchiladas, Stacked Black Bean, 90
English Muffin Breakfast Pizzas, 20

F

fats, 6–7
fiber intake, 7
fish and seafood
    Barbecue-Glazed Salmon, 83
    Better-Than-Takeout Shrimp and
        Broccoli, 82
    Crab Cakes with Roasted Corn-Pepper
        Relish, 114
    Crab Rangoon, 39
    Fish Tacos with Quick-Pickled Onions
        and Peppers, 88
    honey-soy marinade for, 113
    Lemon-Pepper Tilapia, 87
    Miso-Glazed Cod, 84
    New Classic Fish Sticks, 79
    Spicy Roasted Shrimp, 81
    Swordfish Steaks with Cucumber
        Salsa, 113
French Toast Cups with Raspberries, 14
fruit. *See specific fruits*

G

garlic
    Aioli, 101
    Garlic Rosemary Pork Chops with
        Roasted Asparagus, 70
glazes
    Apricot Glaze, Pork Tenderloin with, 68
    Barbecue-Glazed Salmon, 83
    Glazed Doughnuts, 119
    Miso-Glazed Cod, 84
    Pomegranate Glaze, Pistachio-Crusted
        Chicken with, 108
Granola, Small-Batch, 10
Greek Meatballs with Tzatziki Sauce, 67

H

Ham and Cheese Calzones, 73
Hawaiian Pork Chops with Pineapple, 109
Herbed Ricotta Bites, 30
honey
    Honey-Mustard Dipping Sauce, 100
    Honey-Roasted Bananas, 133
    honey-soy marinade, 113
Horseradish Cream, 111

I

Italian-inspired foods
    Chicken Parmigiana, 62
    English Muffin Breakfast Pizzas, 20
    Ham and Cheese Calzones, 73
    Portobello Pizzas, 94
    Spicy Sicilian Chicken Drumsticks, 102

K

kitchen tools, 6
Korean Beef in Lettuce Cups, 74

L

Lemon Chicken, Favorite, 63
Lettuce Cups, Korean Beef in, 74

M

main dishes. See beef; chicken; fish and
    seafood; pork; turkey
Mango Salsa, 51
Maple-Mustard Dipping Sauce, 78
meat. See plant-based meat; specific
    types
meatballs
    Greek Meatballs with Tzatziki Sauce, 67
    Simply Terrific Turkey Meatballs, 64
Meatloaf, Homestyle, 76
meat thermometer, 6

Mexican-inspired foods

Mexican-inspired foods
    Chicken Fajitas, 52
    Fish Tacos with Quick-Pickled Onions
        and Peppers, 88
    Skinny Chilaquiles, 22
    Stacked Black Bean Enchiladas, 90
Miso-Glazed Cod, 84
Mozzarella Sticks, Healthier, 31
mushrooms
    Portobello Pizzas, 94
    Steak Tips with Mushrooms, 112
mustard
    Honey-Mustard Dipping Sauce, 100
    Maple-Mustard Dipping Sauce, 78

N

noodles, in Asian Pork Salad, 58
nuts, nut butters
    Almond Cookies, 122
    Almond-Stuffed Peaches, 134
    Caramel-Pecan Popcorn, 121
    Peanut Butter Chocolate Chip
        Cookies, 125
    Peanut Sauce, 49
    Pistachio-Crusted Chicken with
        Pomegranate Glaze, 108
    weight loss and, 108

O

oats
    Cherry-Oatmeal Bars, 13
    Small-Batch Granola, 10
olive oil spray, 6
onions
    Quick-Pickled Onions and Peppers, 88
    Sweet Onion Rings, 36

P

Pancake, Apple Dutch Baby, 15
pancake syrup, 14

parchment paper, 6
pastries and pies
    Cherry Hand Pies, 131
    Glazed Doughnuts, 119
Peaches, Almond-Stuffed, 134
peanut butter
    Peanut Butter Chocolate Chip
        Cookies, 125
    Peanut Sauce, 49
pears, 132
peppers
    Chicken Fajitas, 52
    Easy Weeknight Pork Kebabs, 61
    Quick-Pickled Onions and Peppers, 88
    Roasted Corn-Pepper Relish, 114
    Stuffed Peppers, 75
Pineapple, Hawaiian Pork Chops with, 109
Pistachio-Crusted Chicken with
    Pomegranate Glaze, 108
pizza
    English Muffin Breakfast Pizzas, 20
    Portobello Pizzas, 94
plant-based meat, 91
Popcorn, Caramel-Pecan, 121
pork
    Asian Pork Salad, 58
    Cuban Tenderloin, 69
    Easy Weeknight Pork Kebabs, 61
    Garlic Rosemary Pork Chops with
        Roasted Asparagus, 70
    Ham and Cheese Calzones, 73
    Hawaiian Pork Chops with Pineapple, 109
    Pork Tenderloin with Apricot Glaze, 68
Portobello Pizzas, 94
potatoes
    Perfect Steak Fries, 35
    Vegetarian Shepherd's Pie, 91
protein, 7

R

Raita, Cucumber, 50
Raspberries, French Toast Cups with, 14
Relish, Roasted Corn-Pepper, 114

Ricotta Bites, Herbed, 30
rosemary
    Garlic Rosemary Pork Chops with
        Roasted Asparagus, 70
    Herbed Ricotta Bites, 30
    Stuffed Chicken Breasts, 105

S

salads
    Asian Pork Salad, 58
    Chicken Cobb Salad with Buffalo
        Drizzle, 57
Salmon, Barbecue-Glazed, 83
salsas
    Cucumber Salsa, 113
    Mango Salsa, 51
sauces
    Aioli, 101
    Chimichurri Sauce, 93
    Cranberry Sauce, 106
    Honey-Mustard Dipping Sauce, 100
    Horseradish Cream, 111
    Maple-Mustard Dipping Sauce, 78
    Peanut Sauce, 49
    Spicy Dipping Sauce, 29
    Tartar Sauce, 79
    Tzatziki Sauce, 67
sausage
    Big Easy Sweet Potato Hash, 24
    Cheesy Sausage Biscuit Balls, 25
scales, 6
shrimp
    Better-Than-Takeout Shrimp and
        Broccoli, 82
    Spicy Roasted Shrimp, 81
    thawing, 81
Sicilian Chicken Drumsticks, Spicy, 102
snacks
    Caramel-Pecan Popcorn, 121
    Cinnamon Apple Chips, 120
    Crispy Tofu Bites, 43
    Smoky Chickpeas, 42

spinach
    California-Style Turkey Burgers, 46
    Stuffed Chicken Breasts, 105
Strawberry Shortcake, 128
Sweet Potato Hash, Big Easy, 24
Swordfish Steaks with Cucumber Salsa, 113

T

Tacos, Fish with Quick-Pickled Onions and Peppers, 88
Tandoori Chicken with Cucumber Raita, 50
Tartar Sauce, 79
Thai Chicken Skewers with Peanut Sauce, 49
thyme, 30
Tilapia, Lemon-Pepper, 87
Tofu Bites, Crispy, 43
tomatoes
    Bruschetta with Roasted Tomatoes, 99
    Chicken Cobb Salad with Buffalo Drizzle, 57
tongs, 6
tortillas, 22
turkey
    California-Style Turkey Burgers, 46
    Cheesy Sausage Biscuit Balls, 25
    Roast Turkey with Cranberry Sauce, 106
    Simply Terrific Turkey Meatballs, 64
Tzatziki Sauce, 67

V

vegetables
    Bacon-Wrapped Asparagus, 41
    Better-Than-Takeout Shrimp and Broccoli, 82
    Cabbage Patties with Zucchini, 32
    Cauliflower "Steaks" with Chimichurri Sauce, 93
    Crispy Brussels Sprouts with Honey-Mustard Dipping Sauce, 100
    Fried Artichoke Hearts with Aioli, 101
    Fried Cauliflower with Spicy Dipping Sauce, 29
    Guilt-Free Veggie Egg Rolls, 38
    Portobello Pizzas, 94
Vegetarian Shepherd's Pie, 91

W

water intake, 7
weight loss strategies, 5–7

Y

yogurt
    Cucumber Raita, 50
    Tzatziki Sauce, 67

Z

Zucchini, Cabbage Patties with, 32